# I Am
Michelle Scally-Clarke

**route**

First Published in 2001 by route
School Lane, Glasshoughton, West Yorks, WF10 4QH
e-mail: books@route-online.com

ISBN: 1 901927 08 3

Editor: Ian Daley
Cover Design: Andy Campbell and Dean Smith
Cover Photo: © Kevin Reynolds
Back Cover Photo: © Lizzie Coombes

Thanks to
Aerron, who has lived my dream whilst writing this book, he and I shared
many laughs over our severe dyslexia. This has been a joint venture and I
feel we have both accomplished something. I thank Aerron for being a
strength behind the book, giving his time without complaint and giving
his calm through many of the storms we have had to overcome in
completing this story. Our partnership is very special and extremely
rewarding, I thank you.
Complete maximum respect goes to route. Thanks to Ian Daley for
sticking firm and for holding belief. I'd like to thank Dean, Nicole,
Clayton and Bob for reading and genuinely supporting us.
I would like to thank and praise Mum and Dad for their continuous
support and I would like to thank Lucretia, Miriam, Melanie and Melanie's
mum for reading the book and giving support all the way.
To the earth, to God, to Chapeltown, Jah thanks, maximum respect.

route would like to thank
Steve Dearden, Olive Fowler, Isabel Galan, Lorna Hey, Kathryn Tarpey

Printed by Cox and Wyman, Reading

A catalogue for this book is available from the British Library

Full details of the route programme of books
and live events can be found on our website
www.route-online.com

Route is the fiction imprint of YAC, a registered charity No 1007443

YAC is supported by
Yorkshire Arts, Wakefield MDC, West Yorkshire Grants,
The Arts Council of England

*To Joseph and Olivia*

# Preface

Transformation is one word that comes to mind. Remembering the remarkably unconfident, underdeveloped six-year-old we adopted and now reading the story of an adult Michelle, assertive, extremely articulate, 30 year old mother and poet. Transformation is a good word. At six she could barely walk down steps, now she dances beautifully. Then she spoke very little (but occasionally with great wisdom) now she has such a story to tell.

Reading Michelle's work produces so many reactions. Pride in and admiration of what she has achieved, some painful memories of hard times shared, and the feeling that this is a most important piece of work in helping Michelle declare at last who she is.

It may help your reading to know some background. Michelle is our sixth child, our fourth daughter (and second Black, adopted child). We adopted children because we already had four, wanted more, but knew because we were teachers and had many community links, that many children had to spend many unproductive years in homes and institutions. We believed that we could cope with a large family, we believed that children 'belonged' to the community, our children agreed, we adopted Claire (a beautiful 6 month old with an African father and an English mother). We had asked to adopt a 'hard to place' child. In those days mixed race children were classed as 'hard to place,' because neither white nor Black families were likely to adopt them. After Claire, we believed that it would be better to have another child of mixed race and adopted Michelle after meeting her four times. Most of what is revealed in the case notes that are part of this text was never made known to us. We recognise with hindsight that it was actually 'Auntie Carmel', who ran Michelle's children's home, who decided that our family should be the one to take her favourite child. Adoption was speeded through, we were later told, because Carmel knew that she herself was gravely ill and wanted Michelle placed before she died.

Friends sometimes said we were brave to adopt, 'think of the problems you will have' they said. We responded that we knew plenty of families who had 'problems' with their natural children, so there are no guarantees. We appreciated the words of Gibran in *The Prophet* when he writes;

> *Your children are not your children.*
> *They are the sons and daughters of life's longing for itself.*
> *They come through you but not from you,*
> *And though they are with you yet they belong not to you.*
> *...you are the bows from which your children as living*
> *arrows are sent forth.*

We were told that when you adopt, the existing family relationships 'break down' and then reshape themselves with the new member included. We were also told that it would usually take the same length of time for a child to begin to feel part of the family as they had been not part of the family. In Michelle's case close to seven years, which took her straight into adolescence. Not an ideal arrangement Michelle and I have since agreed!

Michelle's book has been as good for us as it is for her. It has caused many family discussions and reminded us that a poet's version of history need not quite be the same as a non-poet's. It has caused us to revisit old episodes and understand them better now. It reminded us that each family member has their own *I Am* as yet unwritten. It has reminded me how much work Margaret (Mum) put into involving Michelle in Black culture. It has raised the whole issue again of 'nature v nurture' and 'transracial adoption'. Today we would not be allowed to adopt her. If Michelle had not become part of the Scally family, how different would her story be?

One final word. If you find meaning and insight, and some truth for you in Michelle's poetry and story, then do find a chance to see and hear her perform. Then you will see the transformed Michelle, and I am sure be as moved as I am.

*Michael Scally (Dad)*

# 1. This is my story

Give an artist brushes and pens to create but withhold the canvas on which she is to paint. Then give her somebody else's canvas that looks already to be finished and ask her to adopt it and give her all to someone else's picture. How does she begin?

This is my story, this is my picture. Here is where I begin. I have found my canvas that has been withheld for so long and I would like you to take a look. I don't feel much of a writer for I am a poet, my poetry expresses my truth and tells you where I have been. At last I have I have found my story and I need to write it. It is not owned by anyone else now. It is mine. I take responsibility for it.

I was introduced to the social services the day after my birth. I was a child who was labelled and not listened to while in that care. I was a child who was adopted at the age of six. I was in turmoil, I walked with fear and anger for years, I felt lost and would feel haunted by insecurity. I was too young to recognise this as an emotion, it just felt bad and lonely.

As I grew so did the fear and insecurity, it manifested in the way I looked at myself, my family and at the world. Veils of mistrust and scorn were before my sight, my ears stopped listening. A lot of my first six years was lost from my memory as I was enveloped in my new family. My spirit remembered. I was totally afraid of love and abandonment, so spent a lot of energy pushing away, testing the unconditional love of my adopted family and hating myself.

Instead of solid ground, there seemed to be water under my feet. I was treading water, choking and spluttering, harbouring a deep rage and conflict. I walked with this all the way through my teenage years and through most of my 20s until I met my birth father, read my adoption files and started a trace on my birth mother. Until that point I could not separate my patterns of self and allocate the lessons I learnt to me. I needed to know what had to be addressed, forgiven and let go.

I am breaking a chain. I am using the lessons taught by family, by friends and by me. I am listening to self, making choices and being responsible for them. I want to break a pattern in my past for my future. So I write in the way I would tell you because that is the way I'd listen to you. I am a Leeds, Yorkshire woman, with a strong love for my community and the people in it. I wish for Chapeltown to remember its music, its dancing, its old school blues and gaiety. I wish to remember Terry and Lorna my cousins, Wilmot my Uncle and Gary, Paula's cousin. All who gave joy to people, all who have passed away since I started writing this book. I have learnt we have got to remember our blessings as joy; joy can let in the rain and wash the pain. I have to remember, honour and give thanks to the Clarkes and their families. My name at the start of this book was Michelle Scally. Scally is my adopted name. It means, as my dad found out, storyteller. The Scally tribe were the storytellers. I now walk with the name Scally and the name Clarke, Scally Clarke, for this is my full circle, my journey back to peace.

As a mother, the more I see in myself the more I am able to use myself to the best of my ability. As a young mother, at times I was at a loss when caring for my children. I had nothing but children's homes and memories of myself at that age. It wasn't until I wrote the words in these pages that I realised how much of the first seven years I had blanked out. If my daughter acted like me, my friends Paula and Marilyn would laugh saying, 'She's just like you.' In fact most friends did. Before I learnt to forgive me, this would annoy because I didn't like myself. I was scared that I'd let her down as my mother seemed to have let me down.

\*\*\*

I search through the register in the Central Library, in Leeds. I am looking for my mother, myself. My mother was thirty when she had me and placed me into care. I am thirty now. I am who I am because of my story, this is about finding the missing jigsaw pieces, it's about finding peace, forgiveness and about recognising rewards, all of which, at the start of writing this book, I didn't feel I had.

I want to show you many different truths and many misconceptions that have at times drowned me. For many years my identity has been owned by the Social Services, it's now time to tell my truth.

My poetry, my identity, my *One Love* vibe and my adoption are my blessings, I choose to be a survivor not a victim. I choose to take the walk back to self, healing my pieces, collecting my fragments and splinters in order to begin my story, in order to be the woman I was born to be.

A journey from self-disgust to self-love, a journey through stories to truths through poetry. A voyage back to the unknown self, a walk from child to woman to mother. Here begins me, my identity and my affirmation. This is my story.

## Extract From Adoption Files

**18.10.70** Michelle born five weeks premature to Margaret Moran and Mitchell Clarke.

**6.11.70** Office Interview. Mrs Moran explained that in the past she had been terribly depressed when living with Mr Clarke and in fact indulged in self-mutilation. She had some nasty scars on her face and arms which were a result of this. At this point she was admitted to Stanley Royd and decided to leave Mr Clarke for good. However on leaving the hospital she found she was pregnant by him and returned to live with him in hope that he would offer some form of security.

**21.11.70** Michelle admitted to Seacroft Hospital with diarrhoea. She would be in for at least 10 days.

**2.12.70** Mrs Moran called into the office as the baby is due to be discharged from hospital and she has no clothes or bedding as she tore them up in a fit of temper. Mrs Moran was in a very depressed state and told me she had been drunk for a fortnight and doesn't know how she avoided getting into trouble with the police as she now started fights with other women. Seacroft said they could keep the baby no longer as they needed the bed.

**8.12.70** Mrs Moran admitted to hospital with severe haemorrhaging and asked if the baby could be taken into care. Michelle taken into care and placed with Mrs Robson.

**10.12.70** Mrs Moran was looking most unwell and was agitated about having the baby home as she did not feel well enough. She was worried that she would be prosecuted for deserting the baby.

**15.12.70** Michelle discharged from care. Mrs Moran was looking so well and attractive. She had had her hair cut and set and had some new clothes. The house was beautifully clean. A friend was there who was obviously a lot of help with overcoming her depression.

**24.12.70** Mr Clarke called to say that Mrs Moran had left, taking with her the contents of the gas and electricity meter and all Mr Clarke's clothes. He had no idea where she had gone but suspected she had a boyfriend in Bradford. He searched Leeds for her last night. He said Michelle was back in hospital.

# 2. Adoption

I know bareness. I know the blueness of corridors. I know coldness. I know the taste of Coca-Cola ice cubes. This is how I remember. I know the children's home. I know me at five and six years old. Those early years, paramount to the person I have become, I was placed in the system's belly. The system holds my facts, dates, figures, testaments. I remember in a haze, like I'm looking into a mirror with a bright light shining in. Blurred images, people who I knew were mine, who I have sought to find, to define my way.

I remember Aunty Carmel most of all. She was my first mother-figure, my carer. She ran the home. I was her favourite, the baby, she made it possible for me to love, to feel. The others didn't like our relationship. She was more than a carer. She had grey hair and sparkling eyes that gave her warmth. She had yellow fingers. I can see her smoking like a trooper. Aunty Carmel used to dress me up. I remember a red top, a red quilt skirt, red three band shoes with Bay City Roller socks pulled all the way to the knee. I remember a white sailor's jumper with a gold hoop and a blue bottom. My son had one as a baby. In hard reality, the people who looked after me were paid, took holidays and moaned. They dreaded coming to work, to my home; the children's home. But life is never without its silver lining and I was blessed to have the love and security of Aunty Carmel. I can remember the darkness, in the dormitory, when Aunty Carmel wasn't there.

I remember Sean, blond hair, blue eyes. My first sibling, the second youngest in the home, two years older than me. This was our first secure place, we felt love and protection. We used to play. If Sean was naughty and was slippered or hit with the belt, I used to cry for him. If it was me being hit, in public, in front of the others, he would cry. Sean was taken away, I remember him being adopted. I went to see him in his new home, all neat and orderly. I remember his room was blue and he had a train set. He'd been transformed, he didn't want to play with a girl anymore, didn't want to be my brother.

At six I had learnt to mistrust people. I learnt from myself that I knew God. I don't remember being introduced but I do remember him being my best friend. I had a drawing of girl who was praying. This and a battered red ballerina suitcase were my only possessions. I remember talking to God. Nobody can be the comfort of God; my light to survive.

I remember happiness. When the box of Orange Clubs had come from Jacobs. On pancake day when we had pancakes, served in quarters on a saucer and we could have them covered with strawberry jam or lemon juice and sugar. Going to Ireland on the boat with Aunty Carmel and playing with identical twins. Sean was there. Going on day trips to Scarborough. At Christmas time when the presents came, loads of presents. By the afternoon, they had all gone, no trace of any presents. We didn't know what it was to keep things, what toys were. My concept of toys was being chased by a space hopper, orange with big ears and a painted on face. That was toys. I remember marbles, digging out the dirt in the floor to play marbles.

I remember a dark-skinned girl. She was also Michelle and was like my big sister. I knew what was Black and white. I knew what Nigger was. People would be coming and going quickly. I remember having a big hug with Michelle and then she was gone. I can remember Maria, she had a big scar on her face that her father had done.

I knew what fanny meant. I knew how to make babies, 'stick it up, stick it up'. We played *Mummies and Daddies*. I knew very dark times. I remember feeling neglected. I remember being abused. Don't let me disturb you, a sharp mind, an elephant's memory, was induced by primal fear. I knew fear and survival and now I am on the walk back to me. Walking and healing myself as I give all I perceive to motherhood, to my children. I heal my past through my future. I lay the seeds of my family with love, nourishment and dignity to walk forward.

***

I remember being visited by blood brothers and sisters. I don't remember their faces but one sister had blue, blue eyes. They walked me to the shop and bought me blackcurrant Chewits, then took me back to the home. We knew when visitors were coming because we were dressed up. I remember the day the Scallys first came to the home. They were sat in the front room and took up a lot of space. I was in awe of my would-be mother, beautiful-looking, with hair down to her waist. Rebecca and Annie, my future sisters, had drawn me a picture and baked me a cake.

I have strong memories of the day I moved in to the Scally household. I was taken by Aunty Carmel and a social worker. My mother looked at my ballerina suitcase and little picture and wondered where the rest of my things were. Aunty Carmel had put some money in a savings account for me and my mother took it and said I should share it with my brothers and sisters. To me it was a fortune.

I can see Aunty Carmel standing in the doorway saying, 'I'll see you later Michelle.' I didn't understand. 'You'll be staying here for now.' I didn't realise I would never see Aunty Carmel again.

My little sister Clare knew something was going on. She grabbed me by a tuft of my hair and dragged me along the floor to the door where Aunty Carmel was leaving. 'Haven't you forgotten something?' she said.

I remember only now when my daughter displays the panic I forgot I knew. At first I found it daunting, almost devastating, because I had not been comforted from my own childhood pains before the age of seven and had no learning, as of that point, to heal. As soon as you realise you are freed, you understand enough to breathe and exhale. You are open to heal, you are open to compassion and delight, in your sense of love and family. I'd had none.

I joined the Scally family in the summer of my seventh year.

On the first day we ate cream cakes on the back doorstep of the house. I had cream all over my hands and face. For my birthday I was given my first toy, a yellow Sooty puppet with a black magic wand in his hand. I remember the taste of that first birthday, that first Christmas. I remember that feeling of love, of security of having a 'Mummy' and 'Daddy'. It had never bothered me before, but I was told I should be grateful, and in most ways I was grateful because the Scally house held lots of good people.

I was taken aback by being given presents and my mother was taken aback by my gratitude. 'See,' she demonstrated to the others, 'Michelle appreciates her gifts.' And so I was labelled. I liked that label, I wanted to be the girl who appreciated her gifts.

The first thing my mother did was to let me grow my hair long. In the children's home my hair had been kept short and many times I'd been mistaken for a boy, which dented my self image. The Scally family was full of loving and it was my great joy to be part of it, but inside my head I was thinking I was fooling myself to think I could be part of these people. I started to compare myself, I didn't have the same hair as my sisters. They had it and I didn't, I took the negative and felt ugly. I wanted to fit and it brought out my own negativity and insecurity.

\* \* \*

Including me, there were six children in the family and my mum and dad. Until I was eleven or twelve, things on the surface seemed relatively happy. As I pick up my memory now, I can see I was very insecure and confused. I could not seem to see the way people around me saw. I saw my mother open and affectionate with my sisters and brothers. I saw this easy relationship was a struggle with me. I was selfish, as children are. Only now as a mother can I understand the enormity of her role and how she filled it with her sense of truth.

Lots of times, when it hurt to be adopted, I used to think if only Mum, my adopted mother, had had an affair with my real father, but that was barely possible as her own daughter, Rebecca, was only nine months older. I used to call it 'womb-envy' but now I would call it fear. I couldn't understand why my mum didn't bond with me. It led to some dark lonely feelings that twisted and sharpened in my teenage years, feelings of never being good enough, never feeling at home anywhere. A feeling of displacement. I used to rebel in my own quiet or loud way; whichever was most effective.

Coming from a children's home, nothing was left out like fruits and biscuits, the cupboards were locked and you had to ask. When I first got to the Scally house I was bewildered by the way people lived. Everything was creative and warm. I had come from hospital-blue corridors and beds. We went walking, I climbed Snowdon when I was eight. In the children's home we had a wreck of grass in a cul-de-sac of council houses. I had weak ankles and wrists, so my mum sent me to ballet and tap lessons.

\*\*\*

I remembered Aunty Carmel and, with bitter sweet-sadness, I remembered not knowing, not saying goodbye. I found it terribly hard separating from her, I used to look out of the bedroom window clutching my battered red suitcase and watching the planes fly overhead. I used to think she had gone to Ireland. One day my Mum, stressed-out with all my crying and whinging, telling her I wanted to go back to the children's home, telling her I wanted to see Aunty Carmel. She blurted out that I couldn't because she was dead. I tasted hatred then, it laid seeds of thorns for later, my thorns. I would look at her and muster the whole ugly range of my rage out of my eyes and she would cry. I was in so much pain it used to haunt my sleep. I used to dream of red eyes watching in onyx blackness. My pain was my disbelief, I could not come to terms with the changes but had no power to stop them, so I blamed my mum. I did not know how to ask for love the way a secure child would ask, so I burned inside, craving to be held while aggressively pushing, sulking and storming with my mouth. I was out of my mind most of the time with fear; fear is what drove my behaviour. How did I know they weren't going to get rid of me? I was meant to love them all immediately, and I did, but I was in grief. I was a scared, immature, insecure child, so I showed anger, resentment and bitterness. Life felt just not fair, why should I play by any rules?

* * *

I've always held great feelings of awe for my mother, I put her on her pedestal and then I ripped her down. I could not handle my emotions, I pushed the boundaries whenever I could, only drops of my tears told of my fears.

My mother Margaret Scally is a beautiful woman. She is my classic English heroine, she holds romance, passion, strength of character and virtue. She has an intelligent, quick mind and loves every single moment of her life. I made life extremely hard for her as a child, my sisters and I were like chicks in a nest squawking for attention. I, the middle of three, would classically feel left out, so would effectively, negatively draw on her attention. I would run away from home for hours at a time until I was in my teens and then it became nights at a time. Once I was rewarded, she made me some dolls cloths. I remember her feeling very sorry, or was it scared? It satisfied me sufficiently, I felt worried-about.

I'd nick money whenever I felt hard done by. We use to have a top drawer where my parents kept the dinner money and bus fare change. I would stuff five pence and two pence coins down my knickers or put tissue in my pockets and stick it in there so it wouldn't rattle. Then I used to hurtle round to the corner shop and spend it on comfort sweets. It made me feel bad and good. I figured they must have loads if they didn't keep it locked up. Once I took my sisters along with me. We were only young and we put Claire in the pushchair.

We walked along an embankment of woody green land which

16

is locally known as the ridge, trying desperately to scoff the sweets down. I remember in a blur the horror of being caught. We were flung into a bath and I thought, 'This is it, she's gonna kill me.' My mum was ranting about the bad influence I was having on my sisters. It did not stop the feelings, I remember feeling dirty and sinful, how she must really hate me.

I carried on pushing buttons as somewhere, deep inside, it kind of comforted me. When I see the seeds of my behaviour in my children, it is time to move forward, I realise they need my mothering skills, not my poet, housewife, stressed, bill-paying skills. I try to become tactful and doting, I try to become the mummy they need me to be, soothing their child spirit into calm, soothing my memory, healing my child.

\* \* \*

My father Mike Scally is a kind man, with wise and trusting eyes and a twinkling smile. He's famous, a legend to everyone who knows him, because he is his own man. He has worked hard in his belief of family, goodness and love. As children, he had a raw gift of making each one of us feel inordinately proud and special. He was the first male influence in my life and I have loved him with the passion of his own blood. He would tell me I was beautiful. A lot of my confidence and womanhood is taken from the empowerment skills and nurturing he gave me. I feel his clarity in a lot of my thoughts. My dad is my first male role model and we naturally have a lot of similar ideas. We can discuss and debate what we would do with these ideas for hours. My dad and his brothers and sisters, his family, are very important to me and showed unconditional love whilst I was growing up. I carry the name Scally very proudly for my dad is a writer and my family's love is enormous.

As a child it used to enrage and anger me that he couldn't see my mother's unfairness. Years later, as a young mother myself, I plucked up the courage to ask him why. He said it's because he's always fancied her, I did not like that answer then but now I see that the bond of love they share is unbreakable, it is a mother/father/God union. We were their children.

I also found out years later that Aunty Carmel had come to my dad about adopting me. She was dying of cancer and wanted me to find a good home before she went. I liked to be around children so she wanted to put me in a house with plenty of brothers and sisters. My mum had wanted a boy, but my dad felt sorrow for Aunty Carmel.

## Extract From Adoption Files

**30.12.70** Killingbeck hospital reported Mr Clarke phoned to ask if Michelle could go into care.

**2.1.71** Mr Clarke wanted to know if he could visit Michelle. He said he wanted the baby registering as Michelle Clarke.

**4.1.71** Michelle placed in the care of Mrs Pickering. Mrs Pickering was not keen on Mr Clarke visiting as he was often drunk and she lived on her own. Arranged to collect Michelle occasionally so her father could see her in the office.

**5.1.71** Mrs Pickering discovers a lump on Michelle's chest and her head has some peculiar dents on it. Mr Clarke called in a drunken state saying he had been given the sack though didn't know why. He is having hallucinations as he claimed he had seen Mrs Moran in his house several times and when he had gone towards her she disappeared. He also said he had awoken several times in the night hearing a baby crying and thinking this was Michelle. He said that he loves the baby and wants her growing up knowing him as her father.

**7.1.71** Mrs Pickering suspects that Michelle is deaf. At the clinic one of the nurses there, an immigrant specialist, said that she is quite sure Michelle is not part West Indian, but is in fact Asiatic. This of course throws doubts on Michelle's parentage.

**11.1.71** Mr Clarke called in saying Mrs Moran had called to see where the baby was. When he said she was in care she said she was coming down to the office to arrange to take the baby back to Bradford to live with her and her new cohabitee. Mr Clarke asked if I could prevent her from doing this as he didn't want the baby to live with another man and grow up thinking he was her father. I said I had no grounds to prevent Mrs Moran from taking the baby.

**Later:** Mrs Pickering rang to say she has made an appointment with a specialist at Seacroft Hospital because the baby is quite definitely stone deaf.

**13.1.71** It is suspected that Michelle cannot digest fats. Mrs Pickering says the baby is not at all well and she has to feed her every three hours. Michelle moved to Rachel Nursery.

## *Affirmation*

I am here
I am happy
I am here because I choose life
I am happy because I have God
My history makes me
I am blessed in all
I choose to move forward
I am fresh drops of today and tomorrow
I learn to forgive in every way
I learn to rise
I can ask for my help, my truth
I know, can be hidden

## *Betterment*

Outside of the prophecy
Inside of the memory
Stands, not alone...
Burst of Bright
SPOTLIGHT, HOLDTIGHT...
Child woman, baby-faced gnarled
Shimmering of radiance
Light the face, carries the grace
Stands, not alone...
Burst of bright
SPOTLIGHT, HOLDTIGHT
Smell of warm flesh
Air between her breath
Stands, not alone
Burst of Bright
SPOTLIGHT, HOLDTIGHT...
Flicker of fate
Victors smile
          miracle
Wrapped in the skin
          of colour
That swathes the
Body of owner
Once occupied
Spirit
Flies, not alone ...
Burst of bright
Spotlight
HOLDTIGHT...
(Immersed in Jah sunlight)

## *Who will sing my song (Maya's song)*

Shards of my life, snatches of my time
Image of thought, darkens my flight
Broken like an angel, plucked and torn
Strong voice of a woman, to caress my fall

Who will sing my song, in a Black British voice
Who will sing my song in a low rustic chime
Justify my anger, forgive my rage
Justify my anger, unlock the cage

Shards of my memories, melt like snow
Rooted not grounded, left un-sown
Broken like an angel, no breath to fly
Strong heart of Africa, hear my cry

Who will sing my song, in a Black British voice
Who will call the minds to unify
Who will sing my song, with drumbeat pride
Look not at America, but what's deep inside

Shards of my song, cut you like ice
Listen to the parables, no need for fight
Look at our history, look where we're placed
Three generations, this is the disgrace

Who will sing my song, who will sing my tribe
Who will sing my blackness, justify my right
Do you know my scribe

## MotherGod

Sweet as the sweat
That lines my baby's neck
Lost
In the sea
Of sleep
Beneath my lids
Memories awake
To dance
My ancestors dance
The colours of tribe
Movement of trance
Laugh of joy
Song of race
Childlike happiness
No slavery
No hate

Patterns emerging
None of them clear
Strangely familiar
Reach out to be near
Suckle the memories of a Celtic tribe
Teaching the rituals of our African pride

Skins merging dramatically
From peanut to blue
Souls
Spirits
Dancing
Pronouncing truth

From the hue
And deep in the centre
Of my triangle soul
Is locked
My vision
My destiny
My role

Lifting her aura
She beckons to me
To rock the cradle
Of her sanity
Curious as a virgin
Exploring sensuality
Knowing as a woman
Others follow me

Learning the rules of mother in rhyme
Psyche ready
Perceptive
For MotherGod to intertwine
Rocking the cradle
Turns into a boat
Thousands are dying
Mothers are howling
Holocaust and screaming
Like my first birth
Millions are lost
Generations are hurt

Staring in the boat
With deadpan dare
Grotesque imaginary
Africa beware
Hatred in the form

Of the Anti-Christ
Control
Greed
Wrapped up in genocide
Recognition of the vision
Has to be clarified
For to walk with grace
Not with snide

Gazing in the face of my MotherGod
Tears of love
Flow from her face
Into my hands
To wash my face
Renewing the ritual
Finding my place

Foetal fluid in her tears
Senses revived
Lifting my head
Eyes open wide
Thoughts of the vision
Mentally calm
Walk of the woman
Talk with pen
Loved by my MotherGod

Amen

### *Granny Betty Scally Bates*

*to Michael, my dad, aunty Maureen*
*and uncle Stephen Scally, thank-you*

I know I was only seven
So it might be a dream, a sigh
But me granny loved me
So God much
That me honour her
Till me die
Truly it was my granny
Not in her blood or in paper
Rolled in her suet scones homebaked
In her tears showed she prayed
She loved me from inside
Her hair was white and grey and soft
Her eyes a twinkly hue
Her cuss or scorn could lay you dazed
Her love sweet mother's perfume
Now I could not own a mother
So young so confused
But I clung to granny Scally
Her pope and her disputes
She lived in Halton Moor
You see
Reigned by the working class few
Those who put all cost in children
Those who gave and grew
I'd sit on her gold buffet
I the princess she the queen
She'd poke the red hot coal fire
I awed by her speed
I loved her in her Sunday best
And at weddings and at gatherings

She would control the family with her laugh
As I came to us as blessings
I know I was only seven
So I could not tell no lie
I miss the way I shone for her
I could see it in her eyes

## Love Poem

Find a piece of broken glass
Dirty from the pavement stones
Wash it
Clean it
Find a place
To which it belongs in your home

Love it cos it's a piece of glass
Admire it for its dangerous sting
Don't hold it too hard
Possess it too much
For blood in your hands
Dirt in your cut

Try not to hang it like an ornament
For your self vanified ways
For all that comes from greed
You'll see
Tastes like decay

Pick up a piece of broken trust
Dirtied by smeared lies
Wash it
Clean it
And find a place
To which it can stay by your side

Love it for its trustlessness
Love it for its lies
Guard it from its dangerous sting
Protect it with your smile

Don't hold it too hard
Possess it too much
For blood in your hands
Dirt in your cut

Try not to hold it like an ornament
For self protective ways
For all that comes from trust
You'll see
Goes the longest way

# 3. Sisters and Brothers

The balance in our house was set for me by my brothers and sisters. There were six of us, Annie, Dominic, Paul, Becky, me and Claire. The love I have for my Scally siblings is infinite and uncomplicated. We lived in a big, five bedroom family house in Headingley, with playroom, cellar, kitchen and dining room. The house was often full of visitors, foster children, young adults joining or staying with us for awhile, an assortment of colourful and interesting characters. The love I held for the hustle and bustle of our life rarely entered what I felt for myself. At this stage I was an open vessel.

Of my siblings, Annie was the eldest, eight years older than me. Annie is beautiful, with dark black shiny hair and the eyes of our father. She took her job of big sister very seriously, she would often buffer between me and my parents when friction was rising. Annie cut a very dramatic figure and would excite me. I put her on a pedestal and secretly adored and wanted to be like her. As the eldest she was in sixth form and college, she was highly motivated and spent her time going to different classes. I saw her as a multi-talented, high achiever, an organised big sister. At eighteen, she was like me at eleven to thirteen with her dramatic door slamming and her emotional mood swings. Annie got the brunt of my rage and at times I'm sure she thought I hated her but in reality I envied her and vowed secretly to myself that I would be just like that. Annie was the singer, the performer, the carer and the boss. I remember taking a lot of emotional love she gave me quite for granted.

Dominic, the eldest of the two brothers, was the most studious. Even though he could be laddish and into music and sport, really he was a reader and used to hole himself in his room with his books. He was a sensitive one and extremely dashing, he was our Prince Charming and, as sisters, we were very proud of his good looks and would always scrutinise his girlfriends. When I was in my early teens and my friends were round, Dominic used to come into our room after a night out and sit at the end of our bed and be our agony aunt. He was a good listener, 'come on', he would say 'tell your Uncle Dominic everything,' and we often did. He was our confidant.

Paul, the younger brother, was only two-and-a-half years older than me and he used play with me, Becky and Claire. He used to hold dance competitions in the front room and then he would come and judge us. I often won because Paul is fair. As a child, he had a wicked sense of humour. I remember being on some holidays and him stuffing wet sand down my bikini and I remember him trying to put worms in my knickers. Paul was a joker, he loved practical jokes. He once bought Dominic a pig foot for Christmas. Paul would always be the one to comfort me when I got bad school reports. 'Don't worry Michelle, I got one too.' Me and Paul were the quiet ones when the school reports came out. Paul is a big Yorkshire lad with a heart of gold and has some good lifelong friends in Dave Nolan and Mick Flynn, who always kept an eye out for me. Between seven and twelve years old, I spent a lot of afternoons at football matches watching my brothers play. I used to take along a mouldy big teddy to cheer them on.

I was often jealous of my sister Becky as Mum and her seemed stuck to each other. Becky is definitely the love child of my parents. She was born on New Year's Eve. I can see all her qualities in my mum and dad. She is very much her own person and was shy as a child. Me being slightly younger, and very much louder, worked well for both of us and brought us a sisterly security. Becky is kind, sweet and has a dry sense of humour. She has very much the aura of Annie, but only a sister, maybe, could feel that. She is very classy, with her own sense of flair. As a child I was never any good at sport whereas Becky excelled. I used to admire her dainty feet, mine were always three sizes larger. We had massive fun with boys and knew people could not have guessed we were sisters, unless we told them and produced our half-fare bus passes, which held our photograph and name.

I thought Becky more beautiful and classier than myself, in fact I classed all my brothers and sisters as better, more intelligent and prettier. This was a large part of my insecurity battle. At the time I was unhappy, it wasn't the Scally family that made me unhappy, I just was. I had a sense of displacement. Because my brothers and sisters often indulged me, they were at times totally confused by my lamenting or aggression, 'poor me' and 'toffee-nosed' snob were words used by my brothers and sisters when they had put up with as much as they wanted to. I know this helped because I learnt to become a survivor and not a victim. I can't see my life, looking back, without my Scally brothers and sisters and Mum and Dad. I know that they love me and I know the love I have for them is deeper and stronger than the colour of blood.

Claire was adopted when she was a baby and is three years younger than myself. We both had enormously different relationships with Mum. We didn't get off to the best when she dragged me by the hair to Aunty Carmel on my first day in the family. I'd always maintained it was not the best time for me or Claire to be brought together. I tried to be a good big sister and would look after her at school, she responded very badly to racist taunts. I don't think Claire realised she was Black until I was adopted and even then her issues were never the same as mine. At times it used to infuriate me that she could completely wind my mum up and always be unconditionally loved. That's what it felt like. It made me feel insecure that I had never shared the mother-baby intimacies with my mum. She had never wiped my bottom or fed me a bottle. This, now, I realise, was a lot of the womb envy I held towards Mum. Claire could often sense this and would often manipulate a situation.

Mum used to leave biscuits out after school, one or two each, depending on if she had bought or baked them, Claire used to eat mine and then tell Mum that I was lying. Because I could not control my emotions, I'd storm at the situation or at Claire, so I would end up getting told off for that. At times I hated Claire with a vengeance. If Mum and Dad were out, or not nearby, we fought. It was always to the end where one of us would be locked in the bathroom and one on the phone pretending to call 999. On occasions we tasted our own blood, yet if Claire was bullied by anyone outside of the home it was me who called the fight. I used to tell Claire in our particular vicious times that I'd tape recorded everything that she had said, with a secret recording or on a magic microphone and that I was gonna tell Dad, or that I'd never speak to her again. Claire could never stand the thought of me not speaking to her.

For us to be argumentative was a strain on the rest of the family yet we maintained a deep love for each other and shared many a belly laugh. As children we would despair of our hair. It was quite a thrill when we went for our first 'wet look' perm even though mine didn't take. As small children we would wet or have our hair washed then we would don our heads with large bath towels and pretend that we had long blonde hair like our cousins Penny and Dianne. Our own racial differences from the rest of the family made us close but we were open to dig each other. I used to call her 'bone nose' and she used to call me 'plate lip,' that was because we knew she was African descent and because she said I had big lips. It's funny to think now how we felt these racial insults brought us down and hurt. On deeper reflection I must have brought some of this with me from the children's home.

\*\*\*

Mum and Dad were only in their thirties at this time. They had decided they had wanted to make a difference and rather than have a second car, they brought up children. It must have been crazy for them. My parents were excellent in the holiday department and the family would always go camping in the six week Summer break from school. When we were little we went to Wales. We would all pile into the back of a big Peugeot Estate car.

33

Dad had put and extra seat in the back and me, Becky and Claire used to face backwards down the road. I remember poor Dominic used to cringe, he had to bare the brunt of my parents decisions. When we arrived at the camp site he'd get out of the car and walk off on his own, pretending he wasn't with us. We looked like some mobile children's home.

We stopped going to Wales after the time our tent nearly blew away. We were stood one night, all eight of us, trying to hold the poles down, after that Mum and Dad brilliantly decided to go to the south of France. We'd still pile into our car and drive down. One time, we'd been bickering all the way, and Dad ran over a rabbit. I thought it was funny, Claire couldn't believe it. Dad pulled up at the side of the motorway and banged our heads together. Mum was shouting 'You're going to give your dad a heart attack, you're spoiling his holiday.' That was one of her good old-fashioned threats that would shut us up, relight our Catholic guilt. Becky and I were nearly teenagers the first time we went to France, we had great adventures. When we spotted someone we fancied, the other sister would go and chat to them and find out the info. We became each other's spies in the dating game and rarely argued even if they fancied the other sister, which in my case they often did.

Life was far from peaceful at home with all us children about, but we didn't have a sense of peace being broken, not in the pursuit of fun. I can remember we had three landings, so we used to get in sleeping bags and slide down all the stairs. We did a similar thing in the bath, rubbing the sides with soap, almost a full bar, then sliding around in it. I used to be into experiments and Mum used to buy me chemistry kits. The playroom table was full of chemicals and test tubes. I used to make explosions. Dominic had a tropical fish tank full of fish, until one day when Claire put some purple chemicals in there. The tank then got moved outside and we used to put frogspawn in it and grow it into frogs. One day Dominic and Paul were playing cricket and the ball put an end to the tank altogether.

We had a garage and Claire used to keep rabbits in it. We never understood why they used to die so quickly. Dad found out later that the garage was made of asbestos. Me and Claire also had an hamster each, until I told her that they could fly. I put hers on the window ledge and it fell off and splattered on the ground. She was about to go run and tell Mum, I stopped her by doing the same to mine.

When I got my hamster, Mum told me it was a baby. It wasn't long before this baby was having babies of its own, little pink wriggly things. I bawled her out, 'I thought you said it was a baby, how can babies have babies?' The hamster ate it's own children. 'A good bit of meat won't hurt it,' said Doreen, our cleaner, who was always dressed in black.

Doreen was dotty, and so was the gardener who we called John the Baptist, a name he'd given to himself. He did our garden after informing my mum that she would never find the time to do it herself with all us kids to look after. Doreen had a hard life, she was cantankerous and loud, but her heart was always in the right place. I never knew if the black clothes meant she was in mourning because I'd never seen her husband or even heard if she had one. Mum always had plenty of time for Doreen and John the Baptist, who looked like just like a John the Baptist would. It wasn't until much later that I realised he wasn't. She showed us that it doesn't matter what people look like, it's what they are that counts.

My parents were good at showing me that the grass on the other side of the fence might not always be as green as I might have thought it may be. We had a Chilean family staying with us in the 70s, Sergio and Anna Maria were just two teenagers forced to flee Chile which was in political crisis, they were classed as the boat people, political refugees. They were uniquely stunning people who sang the English language in a warm caressing tongue. Sergio, I remember for his laughs and his fingers always tarred in grime and petrol, for he worked with cars. Anna Maria was pregnant with her son Ricardo when they left Chile and

Ricardo was my little sister Claire's age. My sisters and I spent a lot of time with them. Anna Maria gave birth to a little girl Carolina, I regarded them very much as family, my sisters.

* * *

I think I, out of all of the children, was the most absorbed in justice. I used to think that it was because I was born in October and my star sign indicates this in my nature. I now realise it was due to my family and the energy and drive within it. Mike, my dad, was a big influence in these years. I remember the family being particularly proud of him when he left his University teaching job to start his new business called 'Life Skills'. I was not quite sure what it all meant at first. I was about twelve, but I grasped that Dad often went away to talk to big companies and gave workshops in teaching bosses and managers to communicate and get the best for their company. Mum and Dad were extremely busy in those days and we often had people to stay on for dinner, they always seemed bright and interesting and always enjoyed me and my brothers and sisters as much as we enjoyed them. It was around this time that the family were introduced to Bongani, a Black man from South Africa. Mum and Dad were disgusted with the apartheid regime, and Dad would often tell us that Nelson Mandela was a living saint to fight with peace, to suffer years of imprisonment.

Bongani was a tall, thin man. This memory might be because I was small and everything looked bigger. He stayed at our house for a week, maybe 10 days, and in that time me and my brothers and sisters, especially our Paul, guessed that he needed appreciation, attention and love. Bongani, I remember, sometimes felt confused and mentally hurt by his country and his experiences. I remember it being a huge culture shock for him, as he had been under surveillance from the government and had spent time in prison for his beliefs. Bongani was a member of the ANC. Being so young at the time, I was unaware of the taste of his experience, yet I remember his joy at being around myself and my siblings. I remember his paranoia and his fear. I remember a time he was sure his government had followed him and was spying on him. He did not want to go back and his face will be ingrained in my memory for his eyes, though sad, were kind and dignified. This was my first friendship with a Black man. He was also my pen pal, and our letters continued for a number of years after his stay.

For me and my brothers and sisters, Mum and Dad provided role models for our future and compassion without politics. It took me a long while for me to realise everything is politics and an even longer time to realise I have a choice.

## Extract From Adoption Files

**15.1.71** Apparently the baby has been quite well since her arrival at the nursery and there is no recurrence of diarrhoea or sickness. Matron feels the baby was probably over-fed.

**20.1.71** Surprised to see Mrs Moran and Mr Clarke waiting in the office to see me. Mr Clarke looked pleased with himself, Mrs Moran said she was depressed at having no money so she had left. She was on bail for pawning stolen property and would be up in court in two weeks' time. Mr Clarke had got rid of the baby's clothes and pram thinking that the baby would never return home so he sold them. Mrs Moran said she was moving back to 89a Leopold Street with Mr Clarke. I suggested the return of the baby on Friday but warned Mrs Moran that, if she walked out again, we would probably have the child committed to care as it was very damaging, even at this early age, to be moved around so much since birth.

**22.1.71** Mrs Moran and Mr Clarke came into the office. Mrs Moran said she didn't want to stay with Mr Clarke as he was having financial problems and she didn't want to put up with it anymore. Mr Clarke said everything was fine that morning until they went to the DHSS. Mrs Moran was in a nervous state and found it hard to give coherent answers.

**25.1.71** Mrs Moran called at the office and said she decided to stay with Mr Clarke.

**26.1.71** Michelle discharged from care and returned to the family home. The house was clean and tidy and they seemed well-prepared for the child's return. Told Mrs Moran to keep an eye on Michelle's deafness.

**29.1.71** Mr Clarke came in requesting a new pram. We refused as he'd already been given a pram and two buggies.

**Later** Mrs Moran worried about Michelle's vomiting. Told her it may just be because she has moved and might have picked up a virus.

**1.2.71** Mrs Moran called into the office in a frantic state saying she had hit the baby yesterday and could not stop herself shaking it. She could not stand it crying. She said she had decided she could never look after the baby and asked if we would receive the baby into care.

## *Affirmation*

I walk with my sisters and brothers
Happy and at ease with my Scally name
I walk with my own direction
As do my brothers and sisters
I am proud of them and happy in their company
(I believe we feel One Love)
I believe adoption has taught each one
Of my Scally family the feeling of One Love

# 4. Poetry

I have always been deep: child, teenager and woman. 'Self-absorbed', 'selfish' and 'dramatic' have been words used to describe my complexities, emotions, and perceptions. I have walked in a lot of madness, I have walked in a lot of fear. I felt on the outside of the experiences in this life that everybody else is so comfortable with.

My feelings and questions began to arise at about thirteen or fourteen. I was beginning to notice wide divisions between Black and white, I had spent nearly seven years with the Scallys and I regarded myself as one of the family. I did suffer insecurity and felt mildly alien at times but I recognised that this was all part of me as I saw and witnessed my brothers and sisters going through their difficult times too, and unless I was not kicking off at myself or others, things were generally calm. Looking back, I can see that I was completely influenced and stimulated by my entire family. Our house was noisy, funny, held drama and gossip from each other's lives, it felt socially - and mentally - aware, it lived. The walls breathed colours, our house seemed visual with our parents' beliefs. It was filled with our drawings, photos and certificates.

As you walked into our home we had a poster of Nelson Mandela who was imprisoned at that time. It was a black and white photo that had been enlarged, bars had been put on the poster and slashed across the poster in black ink was 'freedom'. In our front room we had a large framed photograph of Don Helder Camera, an archbishop of Recise in northern Brazil, who dedicated his life to the humanitarian and civil rights of his country. He once visited our house in Leeds and commented that Claire looked like a Brazilian baby, a rich Brazilian baby. In our kitchen we had posters up commemorating the women's rights movement and suffragette history. I was given African, West Indian and dual heritage visual imagery in the shape of posters and postcards, I can vividly remember the days that I would stand at the bottom of the steps looking into the eyes of Nelson Mandela, wondering and fantasising that I was somehow related to him. I remember feeling proud to be Black. My parents made me feel safe, they taught me the speech *I Have a Dream*, written by Martin Luther King. We were taught to be part of the solution not part of the problem. I felt at times passionate and filled up. It was a good but scary feeling yet my feeling of security within my family soothed my nagging complexities.

* * *

I learnt from my mum. Together she and I would attend various peace rallies. My favourite times were when she and I would go to Greenham Common. I loved going there, it was an odd combination of peace and power. We would sing *We Shall Not Be Moved* and chant as we marched in our hundreds and sometimes thousands. We would light candles and listen to speeches. I would play sometimes with the other children, we would get our face painted and visit craft stalls set up by various teams of supporters. I liked being near Mum, I liked the hum of mass peace where everyone around you is praying for wars to end. We used to put flowers and messages of peace and hope and tie them to the barb wire fences. When I talk about we, I talk in hundreds. We use to gnarl our fingers around the barb wire and pull the fences down as hard as we could. Mum is a magistrate so she use to step back and urge me on, we had agreed that I could take her turn for her. We would get completely into it and the wire would be bouncing back and fourth. The anarchy and adrenaline would be rushing through me.

Once completely overexcited I turned around as to get her approval, I met with her encouraging eyes and let go of my hand from the wire. The bouncing mesh cut into my face and my lip was bleeding, a policeman who was standing near by called out 'Hey, hey! My mother's a woman too!' in mock surprise at my strength. The standing crowd laughed, the policeman laughed and my mum laughed. I liked it when I made my mum laugh, I felt brave.

* * *

I learnt to read quickly and locked myself away for hours reading. I would find myself in the central character or heroine. My mother was just as passionate about reading and would always encourage me. That was the best gift she gave. I read everything. I even wanted to become a librarian and did my work experience from school in Headingley Library. I spent hours of my adolescence and youth in Judy Blume, Alice Walker and Maya Angelou. I read anything to do with people, stories, life. I remember my mother would wander high and low and would always give me books I felt helped me develop my own insight. I was given the nourishment of literature and lived in a world far removed from the cold and crap of reality. I believed in people as my parents and their friends were so committed to the fight for humanitarian global amnesty. Within my world, everything that wasn't right got worked on or talked through, I couldn't believe the world could let a nation starve.

* * *

I stared at the broadcast. The newscaster was reporting mass starvation, famine in Ethiopia. I was 13, maybe 14, at the time and in my second year of high school. The haunting, exhausted images of starving people, more than could ever fit on a screen. This shook me. The faces staring back from the TV could have been my face, they could have been my people. They were my people. How could we have let this happen. The last time I saw images like this was the Holocaust newsreels. There was no Hitler here silencing the media; or was there? My poetry started that night.

I wrote all the night and throughout playtime the next day. That poem was *I'm Still Full*. A friend came up and asked what I was doing, she shrugged when I replied. After reading what I wrote she looked shocked, she was about to skit it but couldn't. I didn't care.

I remember showing my poem to Mum, she thought it was really good and gave me a lot of praise. I remember even feeling surprised, warmed and encouraged. I showed it to one of the teachers at school and he liked it, but asked me to change the last two lines for the school magazine, I did, then changed them back. My Mum sent the poem to the Catholic Fund for Overseas Development (CAFOD), a developed organisation over forty years old, which had been very much part of my life, whether at home or in school. It was published in *The Universe*, a Catholic Sunday newspaper. It appeared on a big display in the Bond Street shopping centre in Leeds and I read it at school events. People were actually saying that it was good. Something I had done was good.

My Mum bought me an orange folder with a see through sleeve in it and I slipped my poetry in there. I was also given a book with the photos from those first BBC broadcasts of Ethiopia. It was a book of prints collected by various photographic journalists. Inside were prints of the first visual images to be reported from Ethiopia in the famines. My sense of purpose and self took on new meaning and my mum and dad filled my ever-growing need to know with books, tapes, with inspirations of faith by the people in their time like Don Helder Camera, Bob Marley, Martin Luther King, Nelson Mandela, Ghandi and Mother Teresa.

\*\*\*

My dad brought home a Dubliners tape, my sisters and I lived it. I felt a special connection with the music and the lyrics. Dad also introduced me to Bob Marley, he used to say if he'd been a Black man he might well have been Rastafarian. I think this could have only been thought through Bob Marley's words and dignity.

Music surrounded our life as we grew in the Scally house. My love for Irish music was seeded as my love for Marley sealed.

We were all encouraged to play a musical instrument. I first had a clarinet but broke it over some girl's head on the bus. I was not trusted with another instrument until I picked up my sister Annie's flute and taught myself the basics. My parents were impressed and I was allowed to go to music lessons at the Royal College of Music in Headingley. We all had widely differing tastes in music in the Scally household. My brothers and sister were very different in their taste of music. Dominic liked Depeche Mode, Paul liked Madness. Annie used to own Kate Bush records. Becky, Claire and me were young so liked what we could sing or dance to. The first album I was bought was *The Sound of Music* for Christmas. I treasured it as a child.

When we were twelve Becky and me were allowed to go to the teeny-boppers' disco at the Ritzy's, then our taste changed to Motown and Diana Ross. We met a life long friend there called Michelle. Michelle is a very good dancer as well as being an artist. It was the first time that I noticed my love of rhythm as Michelle would hype up the groove and let herself go. I liked that, it is all of what I appreciate and love now. My dad would write the lyrics of Bob Dylan love songs and send them to my mum. Poetry, music, singing and dancing all flowed naturally. My poetry set its stall and discovered its roots from this foundation. In my deepest and most troubled adolescent years I often put pen to paper when I had trouble communicating my thoughts and feelings. I loved lyrics, the sadder, the deeper, the better, I liked the story in the song. Mum and Dad always read and took an interest in my poetry and letters.

\*\*\*

I was in my last term of high school when my mother received a call from CAFOD. They wanted someone to go to Rome to deliver a plaque on behalf of CAFOD for All Saints Day. They wanted someone younger than me so at first my adopted mother asked my little sister Claire, but she did not want to go. I said that I had written the poem so they agreed that I could go. The whole experience was brilliant. I was not keen on meeting the Pope but was keen to have my say and give him a bit of truth. I was dying to go to Italy.

My Mum and I went to Italy, just the two of us. We were really excited, it felt grown-up. My mum was really relaxed and determined to enjoy herself. I was allowed Pernod and fresh orange, and wine with my meal, and an odd cigarette, although not too much. My Mum treated me like a young lady, I had been waiting for this since childhood when I'd seen Mum and Annie together. For once I had her all to myself. My mum has a massive sense of adventure and we dived in from the moment they upgraded our seats on the plane and we were given free drinks. My mum had never been upgraded and we both felt lavished and pampered. Our room in Italy was straight out of a film. It had dark wooden shutters against cool, crisp white walls, thick white linen was laid on the bed and the floors were marble. When you looked out you could see the Vatican, Rome and the hustle of the streets. Rome was wild, classy and cosmopolitan. The statues and smells fascinated me and won me over. As you walked out of our hotel, you were almost at once on the busy high street that led to the Vatican. This felt giddy like being in another world, that smelt more exciting; it was new. I developed an instant addiction to the pizza stalls that stood like hot dog stands and delivered the finest thin, crisp, mozzarella margarita pizzas that I never have tasted again or before. I even had them for breakfast.

Rome was warm and friendly apart from one racist incident that fazed us for maybe five minutes. The people seemed so tactile, huggy-kissy. I liked their olive complexions and dark hair. I had to ask my mum if some were gay when I saw more than a couple of men walking past us hand-in-hand. I don't remember getting a reply but it didn't bother me because this was all part of my first taste and experience of Rome. Rome was really fashionable, the teenagers rode around on mopeds, their European chic hung effortlessly off their shoulders. Their shops had the look of artistic paintings. It looked like a page of a glossy magazine, it oozed 'the look'. Mum bought me a gorgeous black wide-rimed hat and I bought myself a sac bag, both from Benneton. I felt sassy, I felt like a superstar.

I bounced across the road the day I bought my hat and it blew off. The traffic is mad in Rome, all the cars are small Fiats, the buses are packed like sardines and the pelican crossings are not pelican in the Green Cross Code style but 'get over, don't stop or you'll be dropped' style pelican crossings. I rushed back determined to save my hat at all costs, despite being warned, by a priest no less, that the road was dangerous. The horns blared and I was buzzing at my near death experience, bent down running, trying to nab my skipping hat. My smile grew broader as I retrieved it and the blaring horns laughed and saluted me. I felt young, sexy and grateful to get my hat back. I was in a bubble. The Italian men paid both my mum and I loads of attention, I loved it. Men would ask my mum if she would allow me to model, she always refused instantly. I would complain and say 'It could be my chance,' but she explained that there was a lot of exploitation and selling of young girls. It made sense to me the day of our racist incident. Two men approached us, 'Oh! Brazilian, Brazilian,' they said as they looked at me. 'No' replied my mum 'English'. At that they became nasty and we made a hasty retreat. Mum explained that it had to do with football hooligans. It lifted for me the mask of holidays and the sense in my mum's safety precautions. From then on in Rome I listened. Men would ask my mum about her husband and we would describe him as a Black man for we could not be bothered to explain. It was a time with my mum that no one can ever take away.

I will remember the day as long as I have my memory. I remember indulging in all Mum's attention. I remember taking it a bit far sometimes. I remember how she was the mother that I wanted all to myself. I remember the day of the procession. I remember the long walk down to the Pope's knees. I don't remember sleeping well for my eyes in the photographs taken of me that day looked puffy and I look pale and blotchy. I recall being particularly bad-tempered. I recall scathing remarks being made, by me to my mum about the men and all the pomp, fuss and organisation. We were told where to stand, where all the bishops would stand, how slow we had to walk. We were even rehearsed. All this just to hand over a plaque.

When the Pope came he sat down on his pulpit and rebelled. I watched him and my heart grew warm. He detoured completely off the mapped, theatrical procession and went to greet the children of God - the handicapped, sick and the lame who cheered him like a pop star and waved flags. I watched how his kindness was natural and his smile to them genuine. I walked to the altar with a boy who had been picked from another part of the country. I kept my brown eyes on the Pope's blue eyes. As we knelt he touched each of our heads. I kept my eyes on him, I wanted to acknowledge what I felt was true. He looked at me and at the plaque we were carrying. 'Ah CAFOD,' he said, and then smiled.

The day carried on in full Roman Catholic tradition. Frankincense and Myrrh incense permeating the atmosphere and holding it in its sweet perfume. The lines of robed bishops, archbishops, cardinals and deacons in colours of purple, green, gold and reds. The Roman Catholic Church is like every other church except it is more visual than vocal. Men dominate the church and the nuns are definitely seen as secondary nurses. I have seen this in all Roman Catholic Churches - The Vatican was no exception.

It is very overwhelming in its beauty, Michelangelo pictures in the Sistine Chapel, and the *Pieta*, a sculpture of Mary and Jesus at His crucifixion. I did not know, however, if the presence inside the church was because of God or because of the strength, the power and the beauty of the building. Or if it was the sleep of past Popes lying in their tombs inside the church. I came away learning one thing; you *can* take the man from the Pope. I believe the man is a good man and he remains as true to himself as his position allows. His truth is not my truth, but the man I can walk side by side with.

# Extract From Adoption Files

**1.2.71** Collected Michelle from the home. She looked unwell and was obviously very hungry. Mr Clarke looked very sad but sympathetic towards Mrs Moran. I told Mrs Moran that she must see a doctor.

**9.2.71** Message to say Michelle has appointment regarding her stomach complaint. Matron said that Michelle had no problems with feeding and had shown no signs of pain since she had been in nursery.

**10.2.71** Mrs Moran had slashed her arms up last night with a razor blade. Mrs Moran kept making rather sick and disturbing jokes about her present situation. She said she was drunk when she did this to herself. Phoned Dr Black and explained the situation.

**15.2.71** Mrs Moran came to the office and said she had an appointment at the hospital and she needed some clothes. Gave her some from the clothes store.

**22.2.71** Called to get consent to get Michelle immunised. Mrs Moran had rather peculiar bruises on her neck and was very shaky.

**19.4.71** Mrs Moran called in the office saying she wanted the baby back.

**Later** Michelle had been examined and the doctor feels she may be sub-normal. She has an appointment at LGI to assess her deafness and possible sub-normality.

**Later** Mr Clarke called and said he wanted the baby back. He said he wanted the child to know him when she grew up. He said Mrs Moran wanted the baby adopting, but he was not going to allow this to happen.

**29.4.71** Explained to Mrs Moran that Michelle may be subnormal and therefore would need a lot of looking after. Mrs Moran said she couldn't cope whether she was normal or not. We talked about Section II rights and Mrs Moran said she would feel more secure if we took these rights as it would mean Mr Clarke couldn't push her into something she couldn't cope with.

**10.5.71** Mrs Moran called into the office and said she had been sterilised and they had aborted her at the same time. She said Mr Clarke had spent all their supplementary allowance on drink.

## Affirmation

I believe in my stories, my experiences
I feel my spirit through pen
I believe in my poetry
I believe I can feel and touch emotions
I believe
The scent of my journey is my poetry to freedom
I believe in One Love
I believe in the Lord of the dance
I believe if we follow our dreams
We can only meet
True destiny, life's rare treats

# I'm Still Full

I see the starving in Ethiopia
And I'm still full
Bones are sticking out of their bodies
And I'm still full
It sickin, oh is sicking Lord
I watch the news at night
Knowing as I watch
The people out there
Are crying out with the pain and sufferation
In their heart
When the hunger and starvation
Tearing them apart
Children and adults are crying out for rain
And me I'm moaning
'God it's raining again'
And I'm gonna get wet
And it's just not fair
But all this time
I'm still full
And I'll not go a day
Without my fill
Oh MPs Oh MPs
Listen to me
Conservative, Labour and SDP
Feed these people
You stupid fools
Get off your chairs
Help them all
No more to suffer
No more to bawl
While we're all full

*Age 13*

## Black Sunday

Black Sunday, the day of fear
Her husband lay dead
With the blood, dripping from his head
The pain she could not feel anything
She'd experienced death in the family
They were all her own
One every week, with the IRA
Raiding her town tearing her house
And furniture down
Clashing at the windows slamming the doors
Their voices with mad laughter
Coming to get, coming to get
Coming to get the guilty git
He lay dead, he lay cold
With the look of pain streaming from his limp face
She smiled at him, and as she smiled, her tears allowed
My little Irish man with his little Irish soul
With his mind and body divided, not whole
He touched my heart like no other man
And now they have come to ruin our lives
While their sanity kneels down to cry

*Age 13*

## Sierra Leone

I see a broadcast from Sierra Leone
And I'm awake with grief
Children are shooting with fear and cocaine
Rising awash in their minds
Beside myself with grief
Women and babies slaughtered
Genocide calling, diamond rings sought after
Blood and water
A taste of grief
I watch the snatched up hypocrisy of reigning democracies
Who slave and rinse the territories
Behind your laws of western greed
I say it loud, for I want to scream
Bad blood is in the Empire's genes
I watch you in the news at night
Reporting news with hidden lies
I watch you as you believe your tripe
About your diamond genocide
About your diamond genocide
About your diamond genocide
For every baby born to die
Is the grief I'll feel
In my British pride
The diamond is a girl's best friend
Unless underground as God intends
The images, the faces, same as my neighbourhood
Africans being slaughtered crying out for the sane
Their blood of the adamites we are one and the same
World Globalisation is calling in vain
And I'm still in grief
No more in peace
Till the words become
The deeds

## *Awakening*

It's that suffocating taste of an abandoned child
It's that worn-eyed emotion of a motherless bride
It's that puzzled look of a baby, before a baby cries
When daddy's kicked her head in
When mummy's smile died
It's what keeps turning the underworld round
Ghetto life destruction, culture drowned
It's when that white girl thinks she Blacker than you
Cos' her man is Black and he beat her too
It's when that young hood staring with his Babylon look
Women on the streets not safe from their own blood
It's what keeps turning the underworld round
Ghetto life destruction, culture drowned
It's that feeling of joy, when I've just woken up
Glad to be Black, thank God I woke up

# 5. Sistas and Rastas

The first time I ever came across the term NF was in Middle School. Julie Lee told a new girl Paula Oddy that I had called her NF and she came charging up to me, her tanned, olive, Italian face deep with rage. We started scrapping until we were stopped. I was already well baptised in the fire of name-calling or sticks-and-stones, as it was known, but NF was not a political party often talked about in the Scally household. Mr Butterfield, the headmaster, ordered us up to his office. It was a good job he was respected in my young eyes because when he explained what the term meant, rage and humiliation entered into my world.

It was the first but not the last time I was played by my English female peers. By the time I got to high school racism was popular, fashionable even. Leeds United football mania included right wing and fascist parties. It was almost a religion. The older kids at school used to take great pride in chanting 'BLACK IS NOT IN THE UNION JACK SO GET THOSE FUCKING NIGGERS BACK.'

I travelled halfway across Leeds to my chosen high school in Holton Moor. The school was in one of the most deprived areas of Leeds and the lads were taken up by Leeds United and the fashion for racism. The school railings were black and the lads used to point at them and say 'What colour are they?' One time a priest was walking past as this was happening and I yelled at him, 'You call this a Catholic school, do you think Jesus would allow this?'

I was loud, extremely loud, in my schools days. I was pissed off and attention seeking. I lived in a white world. There were three black kids in my middle school and three in my year at high school. I was told by my Social Science teacher that I was a pawn to the Scally family. I was told by another teacher that we were just 'minorities, and what do the police do to minorities?' I guess I'd figured out by the age of thirteen that it did not matter how close a friend was; when the 'darkie-nigger' jokes were passed out it was me they laughed at. Years later, as I breathe to my own beat, as I study my own histories, I begin to understand the complex nature of racism and realise that the mindset of mentally inferiority, taught to us from slavery, is still holding us down.

* * *

It was at the beginning of my high school life that I cemented my relationship with Paula and Marilyn. I'd known Paula at Holy Name middle school and we were friends, but it wasn't until the leaving disco that I realised she was a true friend. Marilyn was in my year at high school. We had been knocking around for a few months and one day we were down near the Corn Exchange in Leeds and we bumped into Paula. She had dropped a lot of weight and held a real confidence about her. We arranged to meet up again and that was it from there, we were inseparable; each one of us complementing the other, each one needing the others equally. People around us were amazed at our closeness, we would finish each other's sentences. We were each other's therapists, we witnessed and shared together.

Marilyn has the scent of woman, she has the grace and independence of a lioness. She has owned her own walk since birth. Her mind, her words, her deeds beautify the woman she is. Her spirit has royalty of wisdom and a party of fun. Her mind is astute and her thoughts complex and deep. Marilyn is my spirit sister, we cut to the chase. We believe with the same taste of spirit. We have hurt each other in the past and we both, as women, have to work hard to keep communicating, whether it be the pace of our lives, the path of our journeys, the pain or party, we have to work at it. I love Marilyn and I will always be at her side if she chooses. I will fight by her side and always be someone she can run to.

Paula is the beauty of woman, she is from the family David, she is Dana woman, a Rasta woman. Her love is of the highest order. Her life, after years of setbacks and patience, is finally her own. I have so much pride for her, my happiness is reflected in her well being. I met Paula in my second year of middle school and I vividly remember the day she walked into my class. She was crying, not boo-hooing, just silent tears dropping from her face. Her eyes were all black like jet. She looked like a princess to me. I noticed her plaits. My hair was in thick dry Afro-style, a style usually seen on dual heritage children when their white mother could not manage. When Paula walked into the room I felt her presence. She did not mess about, she knew her self and did not tolerate any of my stupidness. Her aura was so strong that I daren't get on the wrong side of her, nor did anybody else. I remember the time we had our six needles and hers came up in juicy red lumps, despite scrubbing my wrist with a tooth brush and tooth paste, mine remained flat and faint. I stood squeezing her arm crying out dramatically for mama. Oh we laughed. Paula is my soul sister. She knows that I would give my life for her. She is worth it, I would lie for her, I will believe in her. The light of love I have for Marilyn and Paula will always be at the end of their tunnel.

We threw off all the rules and were high on being teenagers. We had endured racism, the system and the hypocrisy of our Catholic schooling. I hated school, in a mechanical sort of way, the structure of lessons, uniforms, the power struggle, all depressed me. I did not feel I had worked hard enough and was unconfident in my own learning abilities. I'd learnt that to earn my own money bought me more nights out so I started off doing paper rounds until the weather and the dogs yapping put me off. Then I worked at Bryan's fish and chip shop in Headingley, which I enjoyed, then at Jack Fulton's frozen food shop, where everything stank and from which I was sacked. I did anything and everything, but not for too long, until I left school and worked in an old people's home. The first one being *Little Sisters of the Poor* in Headingley, which was run by nuns, and the second, on Meanwood Road, called *Populars*. I had enjoyable times at both, as soon as I got over my morning sickness when on commode slopping-out duty. I thrived in this work. I worked mainly with Alzheimer's patients, I was able to give and receive, and was amazed at their warmth and their spirits. I worked with people with dementia and they lost their reservations and gave a lot of love. I used to tell my father that the sick and handicapped were the people close to God.

\*\*\*

Joan and Everlina were Marilyn's older sisters. Along with Marilyn's other sisters Greta, Graceline and Yvonne, they became very much like family to Paula and me. I met Everlina and Joan first. I recall it vividly as it was my first meeting with Marilyn outside of school. I got off the 91 bus at the Fordde Green pub in Harehills and met them outside of Grandways. Joan said I was pretty and Everlina's smile agreed, it was my first compliment from a beautiful Black woman and it bedazzled me completely. I fell deeply into their trust. Joan is very much like Marilyn, I think. I was completely in awe of her and a bit frightened too. Joan has a strong sense of character, wrapped in an all-woman package. She has a fun sense of humour and manages to look pretty and beautiful at the same time. She's had four children, three boys called Antony, Jayden and Kyle and her angel girl called Natasha, who left us as a baby. She was pregnant with her first son Antony when I met her. Everlina's first son, Shaun, was one and a half when I first fell in love with him. Then she had Dwane who I'm very fortunate to cherish also. I think I can speak for Paula when I say we became very much like aunties to Joan's children and they tightened the bond that we have with each other. We lived in each other's lives and tried to support and share in each other's joys and tribulations. Everlina is like the warm sun, that's what I feel when I'm around her or catch her in my thoughts. She is a beautiful woman, one of those special people whose beauty transcends gracefully into her whole being. It's in the way she talks, she smiles, she praises, she walks, in her laugh. She never hid the fact that she was into God and sprit, I think she influenced and nourished my sprit from the start. When I look back, I often am amazed that she is only five years older than me as she has mothered me to the same remembered taste of Aunty Carmel. Loving me, cussing and teaching me back to self. Greta is very much like Marilyn also. Greta was the sister who supported us unfailingly. She allowed us into her world, much to the disgust of her older friends. Samson, General's brother, was Greta's boyfriend at the time. They embraced us with hospitality, they sat in patience when we would act like kids, usually me, as I couldn't handle the weed at times and would fall about the floor in uncontrolled fits of giggling. Marilyn would follow behind or would initiate the giggling by pulling faces. Greta gave us the gift of empowerment. We knew all about girlpower, we were the trinity. She would tell us we were bad and crazy, wild, which meant we were good, exciting and different. When she laughed you'd feel on top of the world. We would shine in her eyes, show off and reason. Greta, Everlina, Joan and Graceline, each in their way, helped us towards our now paths. The love I have when seeing them, the thanks I have for still knowing and loving them, is my blessing, my wealth, my full up.

\*\*\*

It was with Marilyn and Paula that I discovered Chapeltown, home to the biggest Black community in Leeds. This is where I found my Black self. I had grown up in a white family and they had told me I was beautiful but I didn't really believe them. When it happened in Chapeltown, that was a different matter. I was among people who had lived a life that I wanted to know. When they talked about hard food I didn't know what it was but I wanted to learn. I proved my spirit through dancing. I won a big competition in Bradford, people were there from Leeds and Huddersfield and I got respect.

The money I made working, plus what I begged and borrowed from the men in my family was my share in our wild nights. We went giddy, literally, when we discovered Thunderbird, a nasty, sweet, cheap, potent wine drink. It only cost a pound but it would get us tipsy. Paula had never drunk before so Marilyn and I spent a night at Potternewton Park initiating her. She whimpered a bit at first with her, 'I'm a good girl' protests but we soon got it down her neck. We drank Thunderbird the nights we were not dancing to Funk, Soul or House. We rarely drank before we danced, as we took our dancing very seriously. After Thunderbird came Special Brew, Babycham, Cherry B, Southern Comfort and Martell's Brandy drunk in local night spots such as The Gaiety, The Silver Tree and The Hayfield. These places were packed out come Thursday with all races from the community, they played Socca, Lover's Rock, Blues, Reggae. Later in the night, if we were lucky some Funk, Soul, House and R'n'B. The interiors of these night haunts were secondary and shabby, the drinks were fine and cheap and the toilets were broken-down, flooded and full of girls reapplying their make-up, gossiping and rolling spliffs. We would go to the toilet in threes, chattering non-stop to each other and acquaintances we met that night or the previous nights. The passage way to the Hayfield toilet was always blocked. That was when we had to concentrate on walking straight and walking with dignity because it was always jammed with men rolling their spliffs. It felt like waking down a cat walk or, if in a sober mood, a cattle market. Taking that walk to the toilet, you were on parade. I was usually okay until someone spoke to me, then my tongue, thick and loose from the drinking, would speak with a mind of its own.

There was always one dead stock DJ who played last season's tunes over and over again and the dancefloor would be deserted. When the sounds graced the nightspots, then it would be full-up. At the dances the high I got was spiritual. All these songs praising Jah, praising One Love, I felt I was in a passion. We three had a thirst for knowledge and these older men turned it on. We were from a Catholic school so we knew our Bible. In the Gaiety on one night you could have strippers, a pool tournament, two birthday parties and a funeral and if you wanted to talk about the Bible, someone would pull one out and you could have a big discussion.

Ronald was very good at putting on dances, he was kind and protective towards Marilyn and was always friendly with us. Once he let us collect money for one of his dances in the Gaiety. It was ram-packed, the feeling of power completely overtook me, I became everyone's friend. Marilyn, Paula and me were plied with drink. I remember distantly getting mashed on Southern Comfort and brandy. Marilyn and Paula were cussing me, telling me not to handle any of the money, as I was giving people more money back then they were giving me. I have a tendency to be greedy with alcohol and Marilyn and Paula insisted I had to stay out, it was the rule, so I endured the blues that night with a very firm Stafford holding me up and swaying me to the beat. It was a good night, a mad night, a 'kick me, kill me' night. We were all donned in Everlina's home-made classic dresses and our beautiful Doc Martens. We went from being the *Vibe Posse* to the *Kick Me Kill Me Crew*. This was down to our Doc Martens and our *Dolly* dresses. Life was good. I finally felt I belonged somewhere. Chapeltown attracted me like a bee to her honey.

We all received loads of male attention, I was hot for it. Marilyn and Paula were much more cool and demure. Paula was very shy and private so we were hard-pressed to know who she liked unless we put her under our Judge and Jury game that we had invented. This game would be played when one of us suspected the other of keeping a secret about something. The accused would be the suspect, the judge would be the accuser, and the jury would be the person who could understand both sides. This was sometimes a fierce game and I was burned as the accused perhaps the most. It kept our faith and trust in each other, we found at this time that we could rarely go a few days without speaking to one another. Marilyn was choosy and held

61

more interest for music and dancing. I could not help it, I lapped up the sweet talk men gave us. I could not help but feel like the ugly duckling turned into a swan. My heart used to beat fast when we walked down Chapeltown front-line and cars blew their horns at us. Marilyn and Paula would hiss at me not to look, I could never resist turning to see who it was.

For the first time I felt I could blend without being labelled and unless I opened my mouth, people would not question who I was or if I was grateful to be adopted. I used to tingle with pleasure when mothers of friends I had made in Chapeltown would ask 'You sure you're not full Black and not mixed race.' Some would insist I was, I would laugh.

\*\*\*

Marilyn, Paula and me would make up dance steps and would practice. We worked hard at dance and knew we were good. Marilyn and myself were taking dance and drama at school, it was one of the few lessons I enjoyed, apart from history and Religious Education. The teachers in Corpus Christi High School teaching those subjects were brilliant, they loved to teach and it flowed through them and it was hard not to get involved. We were conscious of our flare and style, always slightly different form the perceived norm, kind of funky, kind of punky. I loved men's suits and would wear my brothers' and father's old ones. I would pull a large leather belt around the waist of the trousers then wear a tight white t-shirt with the jacket of the suit over the top and don soft, leather jazz shoes in various colours. We would set to town the three of us, to bargain hunt. French Connection clothes shop had a shop called Dis-connect and I remember buying these amazing shocking pink and black, striped jersey-knit hotpants, teamed with a black top or blazer. They sailed through our wardrobe season after season until they were worn out. My hair once thick and unmanageable was now being experimented on, much to the disgust of Joan and Everlina, by Vidal Sassoon and Gray's hairdressing shops. It improved my confidence. I went from having shoulder-length, thick hair, to short at the back, wet-look curly at one side and relaxed and straight at the other. I will not lie, it looked wicked, I was stingin'. Paula, Marilyn and myself all had our vibe shoes. They were deep blue suede, we bought them at Ravel's in Bradford. We would often mix our clothes so we looked alike, we were a posse, our cousins were each other, our aunties Marilyn's older sisters, our uncles were Paula's brothers and Dominic my brother. I was young and naive, I took all the attention to mean approval. I was a child-woman. My ego said I was a woman, my child still sucked attention. Oblivious to everything we had fun.

We were fortunate at that time to live in the freedom teenagers cannot now take for granted. We lived and grew in the era of Bob Marley and our friends surrounding us walked with JAH, GOD. Although we were all born into the community of Chapeltown I did not at the time grasp this as I had not asked the right questions.

\*\*\*

Life from 14 to 17 passed in a haze of friends and anarchy. I was passionate about all my friendships. Stafford and General were my closest male friends, they are Rastafarian brethren. Stafford is tall, with thick long locks. General was small with short locks which have since been shorn. They were gentlemen and a lot of females looked up to them as friends and protectors. I could talk to them about anything and everything, and together the girls, *Vibes Posse* and the Brethren, along with other friends, would party, dance, sing, reason days and months away. I saw Stafford and General as my brothers, although I held a deep crush on Stafford. They would guide us when out with them but were never strict or controlling. They enjoyed the three of us being naughty, it was all part of the fun. In our smoking and reasoning they installed a belief in all three of us, telling us constantly that we were beautiful, different and special. When I was ready to leave Leeds behind I received encouragement and a certain amount of brotherly pride. Stafford and General understood, as the *Vibe Posse*, my need to know my birth father and I'd feel able to talk about it often. In return, they introduced us into their circle of friends and family.

I remember one time when we were in The Gaiety having a drink when somebody smashed through all the side windows in a grudge attack. I don't remember feeling scared as I was shoved to safety by Stafford. In incidents like these we were instantly covered by older people. That was how it worked. Marilyn, Paula and me had a little chant when we were faced with danger, one would say, 'I'm a tree,' the other, 'I'm a dog,' and the other 'I'm a lamppost,' then we would pretend and role-play our roles while chaos surrounded us. We would concentrate only on each other and laugh. This somehow saw us through safely.

Stafford, General, Marilyn and Paula all came to the Scally house. My mum and dad were impressed by Stafford's and General's friendship with us and relaxed a lot of their rules about curfew if I was out with them. When Mum and Dad held birthday parties or dinner parties, and if my four friends came, the evening would sometimes end up in mad dancing competitions between my Dad and his friends, who liked Mick Jagger, The Rolling Stones and Michael Jackson, and my friends and our tastes. We even, in good humour, had Black versus white dances, old versus young, with a lot of alcohol. We all were always the winners. Mum and Aunty Maureen were pretty fine dancers so they used to join our side as the Three Supremes, with another enthusiastic family friend joining in as the third. I think this is what held my love for my friends, for they showed me how to walk between worlds and feel okay about it. Stafford and General are true, genuine men. They don't pretend to be what they are not and count the wealth of friendships as a banker would count his coins. For me, they taught me what to look for in union and what not to.

***

The Joof family were very special to me, this was the first time I had known a mixed-race family biologically related and still living as a family. Mr Joof was the head of the family, he was a Gambian man, dark-skinned, with beautiful bone structure. All his children inherited his look. The mother is a small, long blonde woman with big blue eyes. She had a respect amongst us because we saw the way Uzzy and his brothers and sisters treated her. I remember being intimidated, even jealous of them at times, because they held such confidence in their skin. All the pranks played on each other held kindness and good nature in them. The Joof Blues club was my haven. We were always told we had to behave ourselves by Mr Joof, but once inside we were treated like daughters, friends. Cham was Mr Joof's brother, he used to call me his angel. I played up to it and looked on him as trustworthy and warm. We were safe at Joof Blues, never hurt, harmed or hassled. When I was around the Joofs I felt a sense of identity. I did not have to pretend to be me, I hungered for the family identity which dropped off Malick's, Jason's and Uzzy's shoulders as birthright. I loved dancing in the Blues, talking in the company of those older, wiser, powerful African men. My dancing and my confidence was boosted by the Joof Blues, it is where I learnt to rock to lovers, to wind-pon-man and to exhale. One of the men named to be my father before my truth was revealed was Cham. I went to the Joof sons, Uzzy and Jason, and to Cham's daughter, Aisha, they treated me like the people they are and I would have been proud to call them blood.

We were spoiled by Mr Joof. I remember one Friday night he gave us a five pound draw of Black Leb, this was straight off the boat from Africa. We rolled it up and were still partying more than twenty-four hours later on that one spliff. When Sunday night came round Mr Joof would send his friends to pick us up and take us home. These were giving times, if I had a fiver, everyone had a fiver, and so it went.

\*\*\*

I was 15, nearly 16, when I had an intense first relationship with a boy called Andrew. He held all the traits of a proud, conscious Black man. I met him in The Warehouse nightclub in Leeds, a local hotspot for the Soul and Funk scene. We hit it off straight away and our relationship quickly became serious. Andrew is five foot eleven, with a winning smile and honest eyes. He was always crisp, clean and creamed, and never needed to shave because he had such smooth, soft skin. Andrew felt very grown up to me. He worked in Marks and Spencer's and was four years older than me. He was very good at spending his money wisely and he was earning good money. His family had moved to London and left him and his older brother the house. They had a friend called Martin, also sharing the house, and we would have some good laughs and spent many wild days out travelling in the summer. I remember asking my Mum if I could sleep over at his house, she said, 'Well, if you want his penis in your vagina, go ahead.' My sisters stood listening to her shocked and appalled. It was to be another two times of asking that I received her consent and even then I felt I had let my dad down. Andrew gave me a sense of importance, I felt lucky I'd chosen so well. As he was older than me, he often felt that he had to lay rules for me, i.e. what looked nice, what looked tarty. At first I thought this was really sweet but when he restricted my time with Marilyn and Paula I raged. I began to feel resentment for my stable relationship, and he felt jealous of my friendship with Marilyn and Paula. My rule, in that time, was to break all rules and I broke his heart, which scared me, so I became nasty. I was scared because I could have not met a lovelier man but at that time I didn't want a good man.

After Andrew I looked for a party, I had felt tied down too young and wanted some excitement. That came in the form of Pablo and his sound. They were in their time the hottest young mavericks moving up. Pablo had raw talent and dark beautiful looks, a gold tooth and a streetwise mind. His posse had a sound called Maverick that suited their moods, flash and temperament. They walked tall and were the sounds of our street. They were the Ganja smokers and the educators, and their lyrics would always be filled with the evil and destruction of Cocaine and Crack. Pablo had an older brother called KD, together with General's brothers, Samson, Lynden, Cally and Body Pop, Froggy, Hopper, Spider and Sticks, all men were in this wave, they held the dance and embraced the vibe. Their sounds would spill out of house until the sun rose, where the early morning, all-nighters jammed in our cars or danced on the streets. The die-hard took a breather from blues, drinking our Cani, a sweet wine drink, sometimes waiting in line to order our burgers in hardo bread from Tenner, the street higgler in his van, DIY'd food dispenser. I was green fresh and different. Pablo inspired my poetry and music although I don't think he realises. I remember singing for him. I remember him talking. He was a sweet talker with a serious, intelligent side. His ego was bigger than mine and that gave me a buzz. We all, the *Vibe Posse*, had some wild, crazy, innocent times with Pablo. He gave me my memories, my favourite song by Yama Bolo called 'When a Man's in Love' and lessons, not always nice, to add to my story and grow myself up. Pablo was a superstar, he oozed it, the style, the confidence, the literature, he was beautiful like a model, and he knew it.

\*\*\*

Partying is customed to have to stop. I started hearing stories made up about myself, that I knew were lies. I even caught one man telling a bunch of his mates that he had had sex with me, on top of a fridge. I marched in and made it clear to everybody that this certainly was not the case. My temper blew, I cussed and shouted until the room understood I was telling the truth. My sense of trust and safety felt torn. I began to realise that people watched us in a bad way. I would have people coming up to say, 'Oh, you're so sometimeish,' 'Why do you cut your eye at me?' or

'You love yourself too much.' It changed the element of our night. I became depressed with what I once considered exciting. My wild, 'don't give a fuck' attitude had its consequences. It attacked my confidence and my ego, I felt people were now looking at me to call me down. My part-time jobs no longer appealed and I was half-heartedly skimming through college. I sent my parents prematurely grey in this era. The other children, bearing the worry and the brunt of my rebellion, could not comprehend where I was coming from, causing tension and arguments. I was beginning to feel trapped again.

A friend at college told me of a job going in Switzerland as a nanny. I had to be quick for the posting was in six weeks. I did not think much about leaving anybody, I needed more experiences and more excitement. I was given a send-off in The Gaiety. I remember feeling Marilyn and Paula did not seem to care, I realise now that it was me who didn't care, it was me who was splitting us up. This was our separation. I had jumped onto another ship and it would never return. We could never return to the same again, we had to sail forward. Our love was strong, thank God. I was the first one jumping ship. I left the Gaiety at 3.30-4 o'clock in the morning and went straight to the airport. I was driven by Mum and Dad, my mum said, 'I'll give it six months.' 'Not if I can help it,' I replied. I walked onto the plane, 17, head strong and determined I was not coming back. Six weeks later Marilyn left for London and Paula stayed on in Leeds.

\*\*\*

There will be nowhere else on earth that is Chapeltown for me. I love her trees, her fine houses and her mosques and churches. I love the streets, Cowper Street and Leopold Street, where we were taught to dance. I love the pavements that cobblestone up and down the lanes. The ones that went wet and slidy from the huge leaves that could make you slam down, slide and break your arse, which I did to varying degrees in the late summer nights after drink had licked and kicked me. I am proud of the fact that our park is respected, and buzz to see the Caribbean and hue of colours and carnival time You cannot walk from one end of Chapeltown high street to the other without being acknowledged or wave. This is a warmth that keeps you from being forgotten in a lonely life. I love Cantor's fish and chip shop, CC Continental's food shop and the Dutch Pot, because they have stood there proudly throughout all my years. The families are a part of my memories, a part of my sight. All sorts of races, we have a Carrib Society that boasts Jamaican; Nevishion; Kitishion; Barbados; Monseratt; Trinidad Communities; Irish; Polish and Asian. We have passion in our politics, we have our churches, societies, nurseries, good and bad; protecting and self-harming people. We have joy; we have the children amongst the hurt and angry chidden; we have the adults who cannot get past childhood and are in pain; we have the Gospel church on Easterly Road, bursting with the whole mixed community, lifting their voices to Jesus and thanking him for holding their hands. We have the societies of people who can, and are putting back into the community what they need to take out.

This is my love, this is my pride, I breathe it all in. We have belly laughs, we laugh at ourselves and our pain and grief is as expressive as our joy when burying our dead with prayers and hymns, 'Gonna lay you down by the riverside.' I do not feel blind in Chapeltown, I can taste and feel, I have no such trust outside of Chapeltown unless I am by the mountains, the sea, the plains, for I find the people living in these places also comfortable with their truth and not trying to disguise it with materialistic success or conning business sense. It is only here that my truth is found. I am of dual heritage. Only one part of my heritage is speaking the truth. That one is moving forward with forgiveness. It lives within the friendship I have made, it lives within God. It lives despite creed, class, gender, hate, power and colour. It loves across the world.

Black defines colour, defines Nevis, Caribbean, Asian and

African British peoples - Black British. I am Black British because I have a Nevis father. I would call myself Michelle because I am proud in my ancestral line. Proud of me. From as early as I can remember, I was brought up to hold loving values from my adoptive parents. Although I don't remember feeling comforted when I was being called names, being chased, or when dealing with ignorant, snide people. I was told, 'truth, knew no colour', but I could not find the truth.

I need to be with people from the Caribbean. Names like 'coon', 'bounty', 'half-caste', 'red', 'yellow' and 'scally-wog' were all labels that society chose for us to wear. I guess I have changed my mind a lot over the term Black. Give me back my Black British history and I'll call myself African. Give me a picture of Africa on TV and I'll see starvation, corruption, war and massacre. Yet the picture of Africa inside of me is colour, spirit, truth and majesty the last and the first.

Scorn me when I feel I must be African, for in my truth I have been created of this society to be a minority. I do not choose for communities of Leeds, Nevis, of British people of any colour to be a minority. The history of the British Empire has the blood of its colonies on its hands, and in its wars, mixed in the cement of its foundation.

I was born in a cold country, my blood, my spirit is warm, I know a truth that lives in my soul.

Fear tastes bitter. Looking back on my life, sorting out my pains and all my gains. I'm growing into a woman now. My spirit as a watcher has now joined with her owner, and I feel my times are at one, fitted, connected for me to grasp, walk forward.

## Extract From Adoption Files

**19.5.71** Called to see Michelle at the nursery. She has put on considerable weight and is physically most attractive. It is apparent that she is backward for a baby of her age, however she is quite content in the nursery.

**17.6.71** Mrs Moran and Mr Clarke visited Michelle and appeared to think that Michelle had recognised them. Matron felt that their treatment of the child was like that of a toy that amused them.

**18.6.71** Mr Clarke was being strong-minded about having the child back.

**21.6.71** Mrs Moran said Mr Clarke had got the neighbours to put pressure on her to take the baby back and she is finding it hard to stand up to him about this. She agreed that her mental state is such that she could easily fall back again and that she should establish a more stable relationship with Mr Clarke before taking Michelle home.

**24.6.71** Mrs Moran and Mr Clarke came in and said they had phoned the hospital and Michelle was perfectly alright now and they wanted her back. Advised strongly against it.

**28.6.71** Mrs Moran called to say she was going to take the baby out today.

**30.6.71** Called to see Mrs Moran. She was showing signs of stress but insisted she could cope. Apparently her sister and step-father had been burned to death in Ireland at the weekend and money had been sent for her to go for the funeral. She accused Mr Clarke of stealing the money.

**2.7.71** Mrs Moran was in an agitated state. She said she was frightened of Michelle and she could not risk going near her in case she struck her. Mrs Moran had to fetch Mr Clarke from the betting shop to be present for discussions. He was aggressive to Mrs Moran when she said she didn't want the child. I said there was nothing wrong or bad about Mrs Moran's attitude, she just needed sympathy and kindness to overcome these fears. He said he was not prepared to stay in the house with her and, if I felt it necessary, I should take the child into care. Mrs Moran looked relieved. Michelle placed at Rachel Nursery.

## Affirmation

I sit within the spirit of myself
I call upon she my mother
I call upon him my father
Here I am
I believe in one God
MotherGod, FatherGod, Holy MotherGod
United in one
One Love
We are the seed of that love
I chose to see
What I feel
I choose to feel
For my history
I choose to live
To be born
Born to breathe
I believe that the first person
Chosen by God was a woman
For women births
I believe the Earth is
MotherGod's garden
Is the gift of God
We call her
Mother Earth
I believe the first woman
To be African
I believe in one God
I believe that we all
Come from that one God
So if you call me by Black, Coon, Darkie
Yellow, Red, Half-Caste
I believe I know where
I'm coming from

# Trinity
*To Marilyn and Paula*

You are my back, when times are bad
You are my joy, when things seem sad
You're the roots, the soil, and my wisdom is clear
When you are around, strength and God are near

I thank you for being there, when I am unstable
When life and reality are hard
And I am unable to be there for you when you need me too

For holding the smile, and it reaching your heart
For the joining of souls, connecting of minds
For letting me be all I can be
One part of the friendship trinity

Even when we were young and unsure
We knew the bonds and the trials to endure
We mixed with wisdom
Our knowledge was our taste
African culture, the proud Black race

And each like the form of trinity
Have branched like the roots of the teaching tree
And Knowledge, still is our taste
For learning and living in our proud Black race

I honour you for keeping me strong
For holding the bonds for so very long

I praise you for keeping me strong
In thought and spirituality

And proud Black sistah's
That we be
I thank Jah for his gift to me

## Girls

Steamy milky dettol water
Climb in hot bath
Pick up Dove soap and wash my back
Pick up my Ladyshave, take the prickles away
Cream up my body
Keep my dryness at bay

Well there's…

Laughter in my throat
And a smile on my hips
Put on best underwear
Balm my lips
The tightest, shortest thing I possess
Squeeze over my body
And into my chest

Now we're…

Ready to go
The posse look fine
Ragga rave jumping
Feel the vibe
Walk into the club wid me girls the crew
Yes, yes, yes, man
We love ourselves too

And the…

Music is skanking
The head's on the beat
Sister voices singing upon their feet

Faces alight with physical relief
Time passed away in a dark tribal heat

Now the…

Girls posse bonded rhythmically tuned
Tuned bodies betraying what their sex can do
Sexual provocation
A hint, a chance
Then changing your audience
To the next dance

Hot thumping garage to the next wave
Lift up the rhythm and swing with the sway
Lights gone up sweat come down
Under my panties at the top of my crown

Now we ready to go - the posse look fine
Grin on our faces
March out in line
To disappear
Till the next time

Till the next time...

## *Ghetto Girl*

Well you came to show me
What I did not want to be
Your voice was your beauty
The pain sang deep
It rocked me, shook me, to my bones
You played me kindly girl
You played my soul

Chorus
Ghetto girl, this is not your home
Ghetto girl, this is not your home

Hustlin' honey your hustle is dread
Beauty in your gravel
True thoroughbred
And you could've shook them
To their bones
Like you rock me when I heard your tone

Chorus

Another lost soul sold to the fraud
One lost daughter, another lost broad
Small forgotten sister
One dropped song
Solidarity keeps on stepping as you go along

Chorus

A day will surely come when it's truth or die
Are you prepared for sight?
Are you prepared to lie?

I worked it all out while you let us drown
When you hustle for self you
Let your woman down
        Let your woman down
Ghetto girl in your ghetto world

Two foot square of not much there
You can't sit on no throne

What ya gonna do when your life falls through
Ghetto girl in your girl in your ghetto world
What ya gonna do when it's in your face
Ghetto girl in your girl in your ghetto world

## Northern Black Reality

When I wake up in the middle of the afternoon
And it's sunny outside
I know I'm a strong, Black woman, and I wonder did I cry?
Cos I'm big-up with passion and I'm big-up with pride
I'm a young Black mother, ghetto system
Babylon system
Knocks me off my stride

1996 don't be pullin' no tricks
Reality systematically will fuck up the integrity
Of man's brutality
Mentally, instinctively, I know, that you know
That there is victory in the psychology of a woman's destiny

An' it's hot, an' it's cold, an' it's sunny outside
All the young Black blood dying by the system side
Government talk shit, not talkin' for my tribe
My young Black blood has to deal Crack
To deal Crack
To survive

Chapeltown, birth town, now dead Crack town
Evil lives there along with despair
Disease has risen, disrespect is rife
When are we gonna stop and care about life?
Life from the father passed on to the son
Truth is written and truth is done

Now it's cold an' it's wet an' I'm sad slow burn inside
Crack taken away our consciousness
Crack taken away our right
But we're strong Black sistahs
And we'll sit strong with pride
Have no fear
For Jah's people will survive
Jah's people will survive

## Forgotten Princess

Her mother's life was over
Her father did not love her
Her daughter came to remind her
      of her lover's shame

Eyes like Cleopatra
Beauty of Asia
Her mother could not give
The love in which created her

It never once deterred her
Primal daughter of Africa
For as the spirits walked with her
Her voice grew louder

Man have come to love her
Man have come to beat her
Man have come to respect her
      in her strength, her pain

So I'll write about honouring her
I'll talk about loving her
I'll worry about her, as if she'd borne my name

To the families that do not know her
To the mist that ignores her
To the evil self abuse — that held her
I will take as my pain
For I have come to need her
To talk with, and please her
To bow down and knead
Her forgotten reign

# Time

Listen to your own words sweet mama
Listen to the voice MotherGod
Gave to you
Go by your own time sweet lady
Only you that can sing your blues
      cause life is only time
            sweet baby
Time to cut the chains and evolute
      just a passage of time
            sweet lady
Don't let your darkness
Cut out the truth

Go by your own song sweet mama
Go by the song spirit
Sung into you
Speak in your own words sweet lady
Only you that can sing your blues
      cause life is only time
            sweet baby
Time to cut the chains and evolute
      just a passage of time
            sweet lady
Don't let your darkness cut out the truth

## Gaiety

In my memories
I will always see
The gaiety
Which I loved so well
While young and forlorn
We danced until dawn
And laughed with the rastas
On the street
Those were happy days
In so many many ways
The friendships had were not denied

For we knew as one
We came as one
In friendship in culture in pride
Now the riot's begun
What is won
What is won
But the destruction we pass to
The child
I can only pray
For a bright brand
New day
In the town
I loved
So well

# 6. Single Mummy

I arrived in Bergun, Switzerland at eight-thirty in the morning. The railway station reminded me of *The Little House on the Prairie* and looked like it was miles away from anywhere. My city sense shrieked with alarm. I still had my party clothes on from The Gaiety the night before and felt ridiculous and cold. I was picked up by the husband of the family and went to live in their home as a nanny. Life changed dramatically.

I settled into my new life uncomfortably, my job was far too responsible for me. The mother, Jackie, seemed too deep in her own personal crisis to emotionally support her children. Jackie was from Yorkshire, as myself, and very warm and lovely in many ways, but seemed disillusioned with her life and trapped in her own unhappiness and I suppose never felt she belonged to the village. She liked her gin and this often set her off in hysterical rages. She would start to drink from about 10 o'clock in the morning and would ask myself and the cleaner to hide her gin and tonic bottles in case her husband found out. The children were beautiful but emotionally draining and until that point I had never come across young children who ran their mother they way they did. I had never seen a child physically attack their mother the way her children attacked her.

There would be arguments between Jackie and her husband who stayed silent and friendly throughout my time there. I was shocked at the physical way in which the children vented their anger at me if their mother could not be around. I had no tools to calm them down and felt depressed that I could not soothe them and other times I felt like getting as far away from them as possible. I felt compassion for Jackie and friendship at times, she would amaze me with her mind and her kindness. However, I was definitely the au-pair and would get shouted at viciously if my cleaning or cooking was not up to scratch. They had a thick beige carpet that was like velvet which had to be hoovered in a particular way. If I ever missed a corner or had not followed the right pattern, Jackie would rage. I was also given a curfew of 12 o'clock which I would break religiously dancing Neneh Cherry's *Buffalo Stance* in the one disco in Bergun. I still had my home mentality of finishing work and then going out to party.

\*\*\*

Bergun is a small skiing village near Monte Carlo. Among other things, it is a holiday resort of the Monaco Royal family. I loved the difference of everything. I loved the skiing and the little disco. I was the only Black face around and enjoyed being a big fish in a small pond. I would woo the locals with my dancing especially my *Buffalo Stance*.

I began to think of England as a grey, dark cloud, full of rain, racism and depression. I would spend hours on the mountains skiing. I became obsessed with catching the first snow of the morning and felt close to bliss, to heaven, when I flew down the mountain.

One day in Bergun I noticed a huge band of skiers whispering excitedly to each other. I strained to pick up what they were saying. They all looked magnificently dressed, some had gold ski suites on, but in 1987 this was cool. Back in the village they caught sight of me, which was not hard as I had made sure they could see me if they wished. I was ushered into the bar where I heard everyone talking in a multitude of European languages. I was introduced to the host, Princess Caroline of Monaco. She was a beautiful looking woman, dark, and olive. I didn't click who I was talking to at first and began to tell her, when asked, my life story. This was, of course, what I loved to do best, especially to strangers. I did not give her much room to speak and rambled on, she listened, fascinated and told me I was a remarkable lady. She told me that most of the people around us were not really her friends and said it was nice to talk real for a change. I remember feeling very comfortable with her and did not put any great awe on her royalty. I stayed for a while entertaining them. I recall feeling like I was playing them, acting for them. I could be anybody, nobody would know if I was telling the truth. But I gave them truth, the then truth of that time and, in hindsight, it must have seemed like I had come from Mars, this cocky, brown-skinned girl from the north of England. They were hungry for my experience and I loved the attention.

\*\*\*

I stayed in Bergun for seven months. By then, the relationship between myself and Jackie was strained. Jackie used to give me a lot of housekeeping, and I used to hide the bigger notes in a compartment below the main part of the purse. One day she went looking for some money and couldn't find the notes. She accused me of stealing and that she had always been suspicious. I pointed her to the notes, but from that point on my respect for her had finished.

I had a really good friend at that time, he was called Tom. He was the son of a publisher and we would spend hours talking about African-American literature. He bought me *The Bluest Eye* by Toni Morrison. Tom was a very deep person, I don't think I ever understood him and I think that's the way he liked it. He told me of a job going in Interlaken, a city near Zurich. He said the lady was a friend and had two boys. Six weeks later I said my goodbyes to Bergun and found myself in Interlaken.

\*\*\*

I held a distaste for my second family. Sue and Walter were separated before I arrived but he saw the children every day. Walter was an alcoholic. Although I witnessed him merry I never saw him drunk. He was always very amicable with me. I later heard through the grapevine that he had blown his head off in the Barbarella Bar, I never found out if this was just true or malicious gossip. What struck me was how the rich Swiss seemed bored by life. Alcoholism and drug abuse was an issue, it was only when I was in Switzerland that I realised that they were in the middle of a Heroin epidemic. I smoked the finest of Ganja but I never saw anybody injecting hard drugs. The evidence was only there when visiting public toilets in Interlarken and Zurich, as you were offered two sanitation bins, one for sanitary waste and one for needles and syringes. Every Swiss person I met had money, the Swiss owned everything in Switzerland and the rest of Europe seemed to be their workforce. Walter was Swiss born, he owned half of Interlaken, although I never worked out which half. The boys were terribly confused by their father and as for the mother Sue, she was more interested in her facials, calorie counting and sleeping in to be much too bothered. She was, in my perception, extremely tight-fisted. The children used to scream and rant that they had lots more money in their bank account than I ever would. They were four and seven. It made me feel at a loss in these times as how to maintain authority. I felt at times like a low paid housekeeper or an emotional punchbag for the children. I now realise that is how most nannies feel, and, as a parent, I would not make this my choice.

My typical day started at 7.30, getting the children's breakfast ready, then I would have to make sure the children were dressed and walk them to school. I would be back in the house at about 8.30, then I would have to hoover throughout the house, I'd spend an hour each day on a particular room, which worked to rota. In Switzerland the windows are huge, wall size. Half of Sue's house felt like a glass conservatory and if she saw any smears on the window she would get angry and make me do them again. I would have to finish the house by 12 o'clock because that's what time Sue got up. I'd rarely get there because I'd start to daydream or get bored. Sue's favourite form of control and humiliation was to run her index fingers over the tops of cupboards and doors to make sure they were clean. At 12.30 we would sit down to lunch, which would be boiled vegetables and meat or escalopes. The children would see their mother at lunch.

Sue worked part-time at a lingerie boutique. She was a very fashionable and nicely built. She was tall for a woman, six foot maybe more. Sue, Walter and their children all had white-blond hair and blue eyes. The boys were cherubs to look at and both had a sweet clever nature to them. There was an unreality to this life, everything in its place, everything perfect, everything eaten.

Sue and myself were friendly at first, my interest in her wained soon after I met her uncle who came to stay. He sat in the kitchen one day, talking to Sue. He mentioned the need to get some trousers as he had not been able to get some before he left home in the colour he required. Sue asked what colour he wanted, to which he replied 'Nigger brown.' I was in the kitchen at the time and heard. I've always hated that rhyme 'sticks and stones will break my bones' because racist name-calling did hurt me. I was indignant and asked him to repeat what he had said. Sue intervened and pointed out that this was not said to offend me, it was just the terminology her uncle used. I did not accept this and was shocked that they found the whole thing amusing. I then realised then that it was a novelty having me in the house, a Black nanny from England. Sue had had a male nanny before, this was the next step, I suppose. I was a trophy nanny. Sue promised me a contract and time for college, which never materialised. I was bored by being a housemaid. My day would finish at 8 o'clock in the evening, after I had prepared a light tea, which consisted of salad, cold meat, sweet and granary bread. After I had tided up the toys, bathed the kids, read them stories and hoovered up the dining room, then, if Sue did not have an appointment or was not going out I'd flee, becoming again a wild and free teenager.

\*\*\*

I soon placed my energies into the night life. Interlaken had two nightspots. One, named Barbarella's, held regular live bands in the bars and I made it my business to get to know each band and would often dance on the stage. I became a regular in the bars and pubs, shutting the day out. I loved Interlaken, I loved being part of the workforce, part of the nightlife that held many different races. I enjoyed being a foreigner in a foreign land. It was easy. No time to think, I had run away. One night, I was out with a group of newly-made friends, we were speaking in a mixture of languages. I had become quite proud of my ability to understand and was enjoying a good night, when suddenly my whole front was drenched by a pint of beer. This large, Liverpudlian George Michael style man stood up on a bar stool, and announced to the whole pub that I'd pissed myself. It was like the spirit of tongues descended as the whole of the pub understood. I was livid, here was this loud Scouser threatening to rock my fragile ego. I was the noise in these parts, I had two choices: befriend him or be his enemy.

Steven became my boyfriend, although that was not my first intention. Steven was wild and we had a wild time. I'd been running things in Interlaken, when he turned up I could be bad, I had been nice up to that point. And it was a great place to be bad. To be banned from a pub you had first to go to court. We drove a motorcycle through one bar, in one door and out the other. Instead of getting a taxi home at night, we would just steal bicycles, they were all over the place. When we got home we would just throw them into a field. The police could never catch us because there was no street lighting. We both were running away, we had packed up and our ties seemed free. It was my first serious love friendship with a white man and it happened because the time was right, we had both left our worlds behind.

Switzerland is far too rich and affluent to hold onto street-racism so I encountered a warmth and would often get praised for my looks or dual-heritage. Steven and I were such compatible friends that when our relationship changed key, it became completely serious. My mum and dad came out to visit me when I was with Steven. I had written to them and said that he was like my brother Paul. My parents liked Steven.

We stayed with each other and managed to obtain another job together for a military, Afro-American couple in America. We had met them on the campsite Steven worked on. I was really excited at the thought of going to America, but there was only one problem; our work visas. We needed to go back to England to sort them out. My relationship had by now broken down with Sue, the boss, and it was an equal relief for both of us to get out of the situation.

We travelled back to England with the rest of Steven's friends on a happy, hippie, knackered bus that they'd arrived in. After one of the most revolting journeys imaginable, imagine seven sweaty, stinky beer louts, farting and stoned, with only a champagne bucket to piss in. I travelled gipping, holding on to my piss until we got stopped in Belgium and were searched at gunpoint. We landed in London, where we stayed with Steven's brother-in-law. We were living in a bubble and we knew that going back to our homes as a Black and white couple then our bubble would be quickly burst. We had to live and work in England for six months for us to have proof of paying taxes to allow us to get visas to work in America. I was determined I was not living in Leeds, although I visited my sistas, rastas and adopted families. I managed to sweet talk the Crawley Job Centre manager into giving me a job and became a damn good administrator. Steven got a job in garden landscaping. Times were happy, we were in love, and the money was coming in.

\*\*\*

I was 19 at this time. After a couple of months in London, we went up to Steven's home town of Ellesmere Port for Christmas and stayed at his sister's house over the holiday. I had been sick over Christmas but had not felt ill. We both knew what it meant. I'd had a scare a month earlier but it was negative. I had stayed on the pill but was dizzy and forgetful with it. We did a Clear Blue test and it came out clear blue. Suddenly life changed direction.

Ellesmere Port was my worst nightmare. It is a small concrete town in The Wirral, the residents, Liverpudlians say, have been kicked there by the people from Birkenhead. There were five Black faces, including mine, in Ellesmere Port. This place was worse than Seacroft, my children's home or my high school but with more money. Ellesmere Port's main industry was oil. I had never met white, rich, working class people before. Ellesmere Port was shell suit city. People definitely measured status and wealth by how much money you appeared to have, and if you changed your car every year. The racism in Ellesmere Port ranged from highly conservative and ignorant, to hooliganism and fascism. I had people asking me if I was born with a tail, and one four year old boy thought I could scrub my skin white and asked, 'Is it all over you?'

Steven's father was racially ignorant and thought his few dozen jokes to me were a bit of fun. Eileen, Steven's mother was very protective of her family. Andrea, the sister, is a kind and loving person though she stated that she hated 'all Pakis' though there wasn't an Asian family in the area. One grandma asked if I really did speak English. After Switzerland, this all came like an ice-cold shower to me. I did not realise the hold father and son had on each other. When we were in Switzerland, Steven would talk of his father's manipulation, his control and how much it hurt him. Steven's own sense of identity was in complete denial. He fed his sense of insecurity with the need for more and more material things. I too enjoyed these things, but these were not the be-all and end-all of life. I began to lose my closeness to him, I began to feel like a trophy or a weird animal put up for display.

Ellesmere Port did have a silver lining though, like all bad, clouded days. I made a few very good friendships. They soothed my distress, confirmed the madness of the town and partyed the weekend away to shut out the cold. I met a girl called Julie Dibble. She is a Scottish lionheart. She was not from Ellesmere Port. She was going through a terrible illness, a bereavement and had nearly lost herself and her son during labour. We were both mothers to young children and found at last, in each other, a way to communicate our feelings. We became incredibly close. Julie was a biker and held a great Scottish pride. Her sense of identity was extremely strong and she allowed me mine. We would swap stories of our early teenage years and let the stress out on the weekend, she would tell me of Scotland and I'd tell her of Chapeltown. We had some massive laughs and loved our children with all our truth.

I knew the only other Black family, they worked in Ellesmere Port but lived in Little Sutton. Their daughter owned a hairdressing shop and it became my sanctuary. The first time I ever walked in there I fell down on my knees and shouted, 'Thank God!' They all laughed. As a family, they gave me a lot of compassion and support. I have huge respect for their dignity and unity, they have worked hard for themselves and for others. It is families like these that hold God's love-wealth.

I held a deep love for Steven. I remember a day when first pregnant I assured him I could manage alone if he was not up to it. I remember also saying that he was my security, he let me breathe. I did not want to go back to Leeds and have to face myself. I'd run away, I'd made new choices, bad choices and my children were not going to suffer like I did by not knowing their family. It made sense for them to be living near their family. I had made my bed and had to lie in it. This was my big thing at that time.

\* \* \*

Joseph was born on 18th August, 1990. I had a stressful pregnancy, moving from London and living with his sister first, mother second, until finally buying our own house. I loved the child I was carrying and would sing to my womb and talk with God about the child. I was very scared and felt at times like a pregnant child. My emotions were all over the place. Steven was wonderful, he was very much in love with me and the thought of our baby. Joseph was to be named Jacob but, when he was born, we realised that could never be his name. 'He shall be called Joseph' said his father. It was spoken with so much clarity that it fitted. I was in labour for six hours properly and thought I was gonna die with the pain. By my side I felt something, but there was nobody there. Joseph's heart beat slowed, I knew God was in the room, it felt physically tearing and spiritually warm and light the day my son birthed his passage into this world. The love I felt for Joseph was spiritual and physical, my sense of self-achievement, this beautiful child, I keened for my mother, I was a mother.

My dad was recuperating after an operation, so my Aunty Maureen brought my mum up. I love my Auntie Maureen, she is the sister of my dad and always gave me the gift of self-esteem. She was the first person to buy me a Black doll. Aunty Maureen and her mother, Granny Betty Scally, were, and are, two very influential role models to me. A child knows what is real love and what is forced, with effort. Granny and Aunty Maureen were able to love me easily and I was able to shine accordingly in their eyes.

My mum and my aunt cried when they saw Joseph, he was a beautiful baby. He took his grandmother's heart and we united again in the joy of him. Steven and I would spend hours gazing at him, laughing at all his snuffles and hand movements. He was a peaceful baby and delighted everyone who met him. I would feel intense love and pleasure breast-feeding him. It mattered he needed me. We spent hours in each other adoration, we still do. Joseph Samuel Buckley is now ten years old. He is the light and joy in God's world, my world. Joseph Samuel chose to come to me and his father, he has all our good points in him, and the whole of himself. He has enormous respect for people, animals, and ambitions and dreams to walk with, to grow to. Joseph looks after my soul with the pure energy of his love. I sometimes feel the teacher-healer in him. He often tells me he knew me before, he says he was my husband. He is very spiritual and we are able as a family to talk very deeply. He also holds the gift, the sixth sense, as does my father, Mitchell, and his father before. Joseph and Olivia Grace, my daughter, have a special relationship with their creator, God.

\*\*\*

Joseph was eight months old and the war in the Gulf had convinced Eileen that there was going to be a world war. She worried that Steven might get called up and if he did, what contact would she have with Joseph. It was quickly arranged that we would get married. Eileen made the dress and within six weeks we were heading for the Holy Rosary Church in Chapeltown and everyone was there for a massive party. Just before I walked up the aisle, linked arm-in-arm with my dad, he said to me that I didn't have to go through with it if I didn't want. I was shocked, I had made my bed and was still determined to lie in it. I'd had tonsillitis the night before, and I've since found out that means you want to say something but can't. After the ceremony, and with everybody back at my parents' house in Headingley, getting drunk and having a big laugh, I took Stafford up to the bathroom, locked the door and told him I thought I'd made a massive mistake. We laughed belly laughs until it hurt.

\*\*\*

Olivia Grace Buckley was born on 18th September 1992. I was in good health and extremely fit in Olivia's pregnancy. I felt very pretty and my bump was beautiful. It was a total shock when the doctor told me he was 100 percent sure I was pregnant. No urine or pregnancy test had been done. We had tried a couple of months earlier, as I thought having two children close together was better. I was still young and could still take time out. It had not happened so Steven and I decided to wait and had put it out of our minds.

When I was carrying Joseph, Andrea, Steven's sister, and myself sat and talked, I told her I was going to have a baby girl, with brown hair the same colour as hers but thicker and wavy, as I had afro hair.

She was going to have her dad's eyes and her skin would be olive. When Joseph was born I felt Olivia's spirit also. I knew this next child inside me was a girl. Joseph, Steven and myself, bonded with my bump as we grew. Steven's mother and I were sat around her table discussing girls' names. I had already chosen Grace as a name because I liked it's affinity to God. It was also linked with Grace Kelly so I did not wish it for a first name. Steven's mother suggested Olivia, I had loved that name since I read *The Colour Purple* by Alice Walker and so it was agreed.

Olivia Grace came in to this world like I did; quickly. It was the morning of the 18th September, 1992, Olivia's head had been engaged in my uterus since 18th August and I was told to be ready. A month later I still was. It was early hours, Steven was sleeping and I nudged him awake. He didn't believe I was going to have her as I was in no pain, but I was determined I was going in. At seven in the morning they rigged me up in one of the side rooms. They told me I was going to be ages, and left me comfortable. My sense told me she was going to be born soon. One hour later a surprised nurse coming off duty found I was fully dilated, whisked me to the delivery suite, but had to change the bed. I heard her heartbeat slow down just like Joseph's and I felt the warmth in the room. 'She's coming,' I screamed. Her head popped out and everything stopped. They had no time for any serious pain relief and I was given gas and air. I felt like mother Africa, I was laughing and bearing down at the same time. What seemed like ages but was only probably minutes, if not seconds, later, I tried to ask the midwife why the contractions had stopped but could only get halfway when another serious contraction, the last, engulfed me as her body and shoulders slid out.

My whole body felt like it was jumping off Halton Moor tower blocks. I swooped her up immediately. She was mine, and

Steven and myself cut her cord. I was triumphant, my body shook with shock. I fed her before they cleaned her up. After Joseph, it came natural. The smell of her, the taste of her, of me, of creation, I felt a massive surge of love for her immediately. I was alight with love for my new family, each one more special as my own family grew.

My sense of self took a complete rebirth with my daughter Olivia. The love, although as deep and passionate as Joseph's, was different. Olivia was different. Her needs and her pulls were different. People would not recognise her as mine. She had black, ebony hair and huge blue eyes. Her skin was the colour of peaches. She was a beautiful baby and was a showstopper in any crowd. Olivia Grace Buckley is now eight years old; she has a massive sense of God; she loves to sing, dance, beautify herself and give to others. She is an artist, her spirit is old. Olivia is herself and demands the love and attention for that. I respect her and her spirit. People tell me that she is very much like me, I think that we are from the same spiritual line. I am her mother, she is my daughter, we thrive off each other.

***

I was in my twenty-third year and had two beautiful children. I had been married for two years, Ellesmere Port sucked and drained me. It felt like a two-faced dog town. Steven was going through a hard time because his mum and dad were splitting up and he was sickened by all the madness. The street where I lived had its good neighbours and it had neighbours from hell. There was a lot of jealousy, people in Ellesmere Port seemed to thrive on it. It was so 'keep up with the Jones" or that's how it felt because nobody talked real unless it was about their children. Feelings were drunk, to forget. I realised that I was back in the same boat but this time I couldn't bail out. My spirit was very low, I was drinking to numb my loneliness, my husband and I had less and less to talk about to each other, other than the children; we had less and less in common. My brain felt stale, I felt old, I looked old.

I remember one night getting in a total panic and I started writing, it went:

*My mission is reality*
*My life is shit*
*It's all shit*
*All the smelly fresh*
*With shit comes shite*
*Take shit*
*Are shit*
*This is all coming out thick and fast*
*That is good because*
*Maybe by shifting the shit I can concentrate on something pure*
*Maybe by dissecting the shit I can make my children pure*
*Maybe by taking my shit they will not feel pain*
*Because only shit mothers pass on that negatives on to their kids*
*My pain is no history*
*My mother's pain is my pain*
*Because she passed it on when she let go*
*I wonder was she listened to*
*I beg you paper of the teaching tree*
*Hear me*
*Me*
*Do not let go.*

That describes how I was feeling, my whole self was in denial, I was unhappy and I had to stop running and face my past. This was a dream because I had not asked the right questions but I did not know any better. I was horribly low in spirit, it feels like you talk one language and the world talks in riddles, lies and hidden insecurities.

Joesph and Olivia were growing and seemed settled, I had a good routine and prided myself on raising the children. I hated housework after Switzerland, it depressed me. I loved to cook, shop and wash clothes so Steven let me have a cleaner called Jo who came in twice a week to clean and iron. I loved her, she loved cleaning, I had never met anybody who got such satisfaction from it and I would sit and listen to her worry about her health problems and her family. We had a good relationship, I remember saying to Steven that she gave me the space to enjoy being a mum. I used to take the children to a mothers and babies group. There we enjoyed and found company of other people. I was very focused in staying in Ellesmere Port, I was financially secure with Steven, he gave me everything I wanted. It depressed and frightened me that I still felt trapped. I longed to be in Chapeltown. I used to dream of being in Joof Blues. There was no colour in Ellesmere Port. It is a concrete mesh of ugly buildings. There were no trees or birds singing, although there was a good park, but I didn't found it attractive as it never held sound.

Marilyn, by this time, had moved to London and I would spend crazy fun-filled weekends with her getting to know her and myself again. Marilyn lived in Camden Town. Camden Town is an arty, funky, colourful town that holds a cosmopolitan mix of races, the world of races. I remember walking down Camden High Street feeling like I would burst with shear relief as the sea of people, races and hues drowned me and swallowed me up. Marilyn and her friends listened to me, it felt good to have conversations again that were not materialistic or possession-filled. It didn't matter what colour cream you put on your walls or if it matched with the border or what kind of washing powder you used. Marilyn and her friends would be full of enthusiasm. There would be get-togethers at which I was made honorary friend. We would have hyped debates and each one individual.

They made me feel womanly and openly made it clear that they thought being a mother was an important job and while I was there I felt worthwhile.

After a few trips to London it felt evident to me what I was missing out on. Steven was really into rugby and mainly liked physical sports and missed it badly if he did not go training once a week. Steven was raised in Ellesmere Port and knew almost all of the locals. He was very popular and well-liked, he was one of the smart go-getters who always got. The rugby social scene bored me, it never changed. In the Shell Rugby Club every Thursday, Saturday and Wednesday night, you could guarantee that Steven and his mates, unless maybe joined by the wives and girlfriends, would get pissed. I was not worried by his mates, I was more annoyed at him because he would get aggressive and would be sick. I have never heard anybody make a sound like him when he was inebriated and vomiting. Steven, when drunk, always fancied curry. He mainly drank beer and the morning-after smell of beer and curry would drive me bonkers. When I was pregnant with Joe and Olivia, it made me physically sick, the odour of the bathroom and bedroom, not to mention his breath. If not pregnant I was more into whisky, shots or liquors and a nice spliff, which probably did not smell too good either. Steven and I had a passionate, stressful relationship. My love for him was very deep, it will always be there because I see his nature and his smile in our children.

Physically and mentally I was beginning to recover from pregnancy and enjoy life again. Joe and Olivia were happy and thriving. Olivia was sleeping well throughout the night. They were good babies in the sense they were adored, had lots of attention and few health and worry issues. Julie and I spent loads of time in each other's company and, as Julie was older than myself, I felt I needed the advice and support she gave. Julie had two children, Jake and Molly, who were each nine months younger than my two. I became very close to Jake and Molly as Julie was close to mine. We were both bored with the rugby scene, Julie's husband Andy played too, and we began to go to Chester religiously every Friday night. We looked forward to our girlie nights. We'd spend half the week discussing what we were gonna be wearing and so on. We took our attitude from our spouses; work hard, play hard. We filled the children's days up with activities and made sure there was food on the table and the bills were paid. Then on Fridays we hit Chester. It was brilliant. We would spend hours getting ready, hiding our lumps and bumps and we always had a bottle of wine to sip from as we transformed ourselves to young women. I looked forward all week to these Fridays. Once out, we stayed in each other's company, chatting, talking, and mingling with anybody who sought to talk to us both. Julie is strong-hearted and strong-minded, her cuss and remarks could sting as they could please. We spent many a Friday night giggling and sending away men, confident in what we were doing out. This was our place and we enjoyed it. We would dance the night away. I enjoy being around people and talking, I felt able to get through again, be young and be me again, as long as I had my friendship with Julie and our nights out.

\*\*\*

Steven and I muddled along in our everyday life, things were happening and changing fast. My love for Steven had been needy and emotional while the children were babies. My newfound confidence, I think, made him uneasy. I felt he did not know where I was coming from. Everything about our situation, our living together, as Olivia's first birthday and her christening dawned, was difficult. Steven was working harder and harder as his business turned over. He was at breaking point sometimes. I was twenty-three and felt abandoned at times. My only lifeline was Julie, unless I phoned mum or Marilyn, but when I did that it increased my loneliness as they were so sympathetic and supportive. My mum understood my depression. I remember her shuddering at the lack of life and vitality in Ellesmere Port once when she came to visit me. When I say it is a concrete mile I'm telling no lie. Mum had brought me up in a multitude of people, situations and lives. I could be sat at the Scally house for two days and would be introduced to people who were from more walks of life, and learn and listen. I never felt like that in Ellesmere Port.

Steven's mum and dad were going through an emotional separation. Melvyn, Steven's dad, had been having an affair. This really shook Steven up and I was conscious of how much it was hurting him. Steven's mum had been 100% devoted to her children and her marriage. Eileen was a very bright and intelligent woman, she had a great loyalty and lived for her family. I could feel her anguish as, at first, she was naturally devastated by her husband's deception and Steven and me were bewildered as to how to give her the right support. Andrea, throughout this time, was a rock, giving solid support to her mother, father and brother. It was hard to comprehend after a 25 year relationship. I could not understand Melyvn's morals. The stress and the anxiety of the situation spilled over to our fragile young love, our young family. It began by sly quotes said by Steven such as, 'You can dress a pig up but it's still a pig,' said in fun of course. Or if I had spent the Friday preparing to go out - which meant me bathing the children - preparing the evening meal, he'd have an argument with me or I with him over really stupid things. He'd want to make love with me as soon as I was ready to go out the door or, if we by chance happened to go out together, he'd want to come straight back. He'd be questioning and difficult when I got back from my night out. His rugby life became his way out, we began to move apart. I remember shocking my Scally family and friends by saying that I loved Steven but was no longer in love with him. I remember coming to stay from Leeds and persistently reassuring him that I was definitely not getting off with any white man, as there were no Black men in Ellesmere Port or Chester that I knew. I felt distant from him in our relationship.

We used to be a team fighting and maintaining our relationship, but it felt now like we were on opposite sides. I was on a rollercoaster of depression, I clung to the belief that my children were too young to need me to be the wild and crazy child that I felt that I was. I tried to be the mother I'd always dreamed of being and was burnt by my guilt of not being able enough. As the arguments grew and the aggression rose, the more we lost respect for each other. Our arguments became weekly and resentful. I felt trapped in our relationship and understood what the saying 'bird in a cage' felt like.

A month or so before the break-up of our marriage, I went home to visit my family. Claire, Rebecca and me spent a day together at a spiritual fete held at the Merrion Hotel, Leeds. There were teams of people there participating and going for readings. There was a wide choice of healers, clairvoyants, palm readers, astrologers, psychics and tarot card readers. I sat firmly down, drawn to a clairvoyant who also used tarot reading as well. She advised me to get out of my situation immediately otherwise there would be heartache and trouble and that, if I saw a way out I would and could be happy and secure. I did not want to see what the clairvoyant saw as I knew my relationship was going from bad to worse and could not control the rolling events from becoming a catastrophe. I came away from the fete feeling a little relieved but mainly confused. On one hand, the confirmation that my marriage was in trouble and affirmed by someone I didn't know me made me feel secure, like I wasn't imagining it or making it up. It was very hard to verbalise properly how I was feeling, my helplessness of what to actually do in my predicament and my emotional and financial insecurity. The thought of leaving worried me. Steven had always assured me that I'd never be able to take the kids if I left. He felt more powerful and worldly-wise than me and I believed in him. Steven was such a loving father to his children when he was around, that I felt dirty and condemned, selfish when I even dreamed about it. Yet fate is always watching and waiting, it holds fears and insecurities. What goes around comes around more painfully, with more distress. My telling signs were there, yet my eyes were blind the fortnight before Steven and I split up.

Steven was bored with my 'poor me' attitude, he was at the end of his compassion. He provided for me and I still was not happy. He began to immerse himself in sport and work leaving nil free time for his family. This caused a lot of mis-communication. One day he arrived home at six in the morning. He was loaded, drunk with beer and had lost his key. I was long gone, asleep in my bed. Through my snoring I heard commotion at the back of the house. I was gripped with fear on awaking and carried Steven's baseball bat downstairs. I saw the figure of a man trying to get into my back lounge window and I kicked off, I fought violently in the dark. It was Steven. He damaged my hand before I realised who it was. I thought we were having a break in. I could not understand why he had come through the back way, nevertheless this was the most fierce encounter we'd had with each other and we were both sensitive, shocked, had wounded egos. We also realised with love and fear what we both might lose.

\*\*\*

Steven suggested that I have my hair plaited, one of Steven's qualities was that if he felt in the wrong he'd pay out generously. Steven knew me and knew a different hairstyle could propel me out of self-depression to become a new person, maybe another image which I could hide behind. Paula from 'Charisma' was plaiting my hair, it took a long time because I had requested the plaits long and fine. Steven and I had been treading on eggshells since his back window entrance and I felt that we both knew we had crossed that line but did not want to get to the end of it.

My hair appointment finished at 10.30 in the evening, I'd been there since 9.00 that morning. Once my hair was finished, I went to meet Steven, who I'd arranged to meet at 9.00pm. I was buzzing at my new look and rushed to catch him. I'd arranged to go to Chester clubbing with Julie that night and was worried that Steven may be annoyed because it was nearly last orders. I remember feeling relieved when finally I saw him. He told me I looked beautiful and was warm and attentive to me, kissing and cuddling me. I remember thinking romantically to myself that somehow we had got over our rough patch. I felt new and glamorous, I felt happy that night. Steven gave me some money and told me to have a good night in Chester with Julie and we parted that night looking forward to meeting up with each other later at home. I was high in my good fortunes, my troubles and worries seemed far behind me.

I knocked on Julie's back door feeling destined to have the night of nights. Our evening started with a bang, we were celebrating life and drinking Jack Daniel's. Julie had lived in Chester before she met her husband and still knew lots of people. That night we met a group of her old drinking buddies, they were a flashy set of interesting people and they'd just been to Chester horse races and were buzzing from their day. We sat about talking, drinking, and we were dancing. Just like in Camden Town these people displayed status and confidence, our conversations that night stimulated intellectually. One of the women, Anna, was a manager at a battered wife's hostel, we spent most of the night talking as I was interested in working with people again. I stuffed her number down my bra, and we joined in the merriment. It was the first ever night that Julie and myself had not stuck by each other's side, we were so busy talking drinking and enjoying ourselves.

At 3.00, the club shut at 3.30, I realised that I had completely lost Julie. I began to panic. I badly wanted to get home to Steven but was too drunk to think clearly and was scared he'd kick off or we'd have a repeat performance of out last bout. I'd handed all my keys and money to Julie as she was carrying the bag. Julie's friends offered me a lift back to their hotel to get me some more cash so I could get home. Ellesmere Port is nine miles from

Chester. I was pleased and felt grateful that they could help me out like this. I was having much too much fun with them to want to leave, we went back to the hotel and enjoyed a makeshift party. I awoke or regained conciseness at 6.30 that morning with a heavy hangover and a sense of dread.

Julie's friends panicked when they realised my sense of alarm, each offered to ring home and explain what had happened. I shrugged them off sensing explanation was too late. I arrived home. The sun was shining, my head was coldly thudding from the alcohol I had consumed. My sense alerted me to my imminent danger, my body rigid with fear. I knew Steven wouldn't let me explain. I remember the taxi turning into the street, by now I was loudly babbling, verbalising my panic. The taxi driver seemed eager to get me out of his car. He did not need to fret as Steven was waiting outside the house. He flung open the taxi door and gripped me by the hair, the newly plaited, extended hair, dragged me up the garden and threw me indoors where hell reigned. Somewhere in this madness I remember the feeling of everything slowing down, I felt sorry for him throughout the remarks, punches and slaps. Steven's face was yellow-white with worry. He'd been out with his mates so he was drunk, angry too. Most of his anger came through in accusations of betrayal. I refused to understand this because when I was in Leeds, London and Switzerland I never came in before seven in the morning. I was a Blues girl and presumed we had an understanding. It was a Friday night so it was Steven's turn to stay in, if he didn't want to he would ask our baby-sitter, always a friend of the family. I did feel guilty and sinful when he punched me on the nose in Joseph's bedroom and it began to bleed all over the white shirt I was wearing. I felt shabby and selfish when I looked at my son's eyes. It was a look my memory can not get over. I had passed it onto my son. I was being beaten and in frustration my whole self mourned. With my rage and the little alcohol I had left in my body, I flew to the phone and screamed down the line, 'Dad, he's gonna kill me!' My dad said he'd come and pick me up. I remember screaming down the phone at Julie's husband, 'You've got what you wanted.' My secret fear had been that none of them liked me, no one but Julie, and I'd felt an indifference to her too which made my feelings run true. I have always been able to look up to Julie for her intelligence and mind, her good heart and soul. She was heartbroken at the turn of events and had merely been pissed and gone home.

\* \* \*

I remember with bile sickness my utter humiliation and devastation when my dad walked through the punched broken doors of my house. My sense of complete failure, madness and fear. I could not believe it had happened or ended like this. I had blood all over my clothes and my face was throbbing and numb, I felt worthless. I remember feeling too ashamed to look at Dad. I had let my children down. I was in a daze, I knew I was never going back and that this was my escape from that place. I felt like the ugly adopted six-year-old, the one I'd left behind, ran away from, disgrace and guilt ripped through my body. I sat clinging to my children, Dad stopped off at some shops and bought me some cigs, his kindness reminded me of our Paul. Tearful and trembling from shock we drove back to Leeds.

When we arrived back at the Scally house there was a hum of disbelief throughout from Mum, my brothers and sisters. I could not bare their shock at a time like this, I was so dazed and reeling from the turn of events. I felt needy and wanted to be made a fuss of. They seemed to me to be taking it lightly, I should not have stayed out. I felt they, better than anyone, should know me. I could not accept my blame while covered with his bruises. I was angry, Mum made a comment one day about the fact that a lot of women go through violence much worse than me. I felt like she said I'd asked for it. I was swimming in pain, I was afraid of what I was going to do next. In the end, the choice was made for me when, one night, I stayed out later than promised. Mum was furious and said I was selfish and reminded me of my children. I was hurt but this now seemed normal, I could not understand how Mum could not understand how devastated I was. I felt crushed by the whole situation. I lasted at the Scally's for one week until I rented some property in Harehills, Leeds.

Steven was very remorseful, but, despite being part of their lives for five years, his parents and family did not ring me once. His father took him on holiday to get over it. Steven wrote me a letter saying that he'd been unfaithful during our marriage and that's why he became so jealous. But by then it didn't matter. I just needed his money to raise the children.

My friends, Marilyn and Paula, were by my side the very next day. General and Stafford were also there. I remember Shaun and Dwayne, Everlina's boys, being so happy to see me. My Auntie Maureen gave me strength and listened with an experienced ear, she never made me feel like I was talking rubbish.

I asked my father to confront Steven about what had happened that day. I wanted him to shout and rage at Steve for hitting his daughter. My dad's a communicator, he listened patiently to Steven for what seemed hours, no raised voice, no how dare you. I felt he had not protected me because my feelings of hurt translated to anger, my anger, my pain. My Black friends gathered round me and Paula and her long-time boyfriend Billy moved in and carried my children. In those first few months I was manic, I would drink to dull the pain. Friends watched and tried to tell me but I did not like myself, I hated myself. Here I was back in Leeds, I felt a fraud, I wore a big false smile and started to work in Harvey's, a wine bar in the city.

I soon realised how financially spoilt I had been with Steven. I took Joseph and Olivia up to Roundhay Park and ordered them some orange juice and biscuits. The bill came to nearly five pounds. I went in my purse and it wasn't there. I'd never been short of money with Steven. I wondered why I couldn't have been shallower, everyone else seemed to cope. Walking out on a marriage is very difficult and I was never brave enough. I did feel guilty for being ungrateful, Steven tried his utmost for me, but I was very difficult to live with. If I had stayed on living there, I would have been an alcoholic.

* * *

The role of a mother is as the earth, it is enriched bred of soul labour and seed, one of which comes from God and is called love. My role as a mother comes within my pure being. The one I talk and pray with. It also comes with guilt or with the need to forgive myself in order to learn. I know who I am. At the end of my truth, my nurturing and acceptance of each of my child's spirits is the utmost lesson I do accept, a revelation of God by which I am humbled and blessed.

# Extract From Adoption Files

**21.7.71** Letter from Miss Howe to say Section II rights were confirmed on June 22nd. Michelle had earache on return from home. She is not reaching the stages of development she should be according to her chronological age.

**26.7.71** Mrs Moran handed me a letter from Mr Clarke, it was headed Armley Prison. He was taken in for failing to maintain his previous cohabitee and six children. I explained about Section II.

**26.8.71** *Report.* Health – very large, deafness was due to mucus in her ears. Can hear now. Slow, lazy, but is beginning to be more alert since operation on ears. Summary – lack of progress gives great cause for concern, wonder if there is some metabolic disorder. Both her parents are of very low intelligence. Mrs Moran was drunk throughout her pregnancy. While Michelle was at home, Mrs Moran gave her very little stimulus, just picked her up to feed her.

**4.9.71** Mr Clarke called wanting the baby back. I explained she is now in the care of the local authority and that was not possible by mere request. Mr Clarke would not accept this and left saying he would get her back somehow.

**13.9.71** Phone call wanting to clarify if the three other Moran children were aware of Michelle's existence. I said I thought this hadn't been mentioned.

**14.10.71** Mrs Moran was admitted to hospital and threatening suicide.

**21.10.71** Doctor feels that Michelle's slow development is due to laziness and nothing more.

**4.11.71** Mrs Moran called from hospital and asked if I could tell Mr Clarke where she was and for him to bring some night clothes. I visited Mr Clarke who was sweeping up broken glass. Mrs Moran had apparently taken some tablets and drunk wine on top of it and then smashed all the glasses in the house and the armchair. Mr Clarke has an affection for Mrs Moran but cannot comprehend she is mentally ill.

**13.1.72** Visited Rachel Nursery, Michelle is a very attractive child. Her response was nil at first, but after we had played she started to show some interest.

## Affirmation

I affirm the love and beauty of my children
I affirm my awe and myself in God
I am a mother, a shepherd of God's children
I am in forgiveness of myself and others
I am a friend to myself
Sometimes wild
Sometimes peaceful
Like the complexities
Of Mother Earth herself
Here I am
I am a good mother
Each stone I stepped led me here

## Too Late

A whisper of forgiveness
In the second of too late
A vague yet distant thunder
Volcanic boiled to quake
Anger swirls around my presence
Bugging at my seams
Choking on the restrain
I hold it throttle it
I bleed
Don't go
I want to scream with panic
In the second of too late
He's gone
My anger leaves me weeping
Mourning my fate
Time and tides have ripped us
Carved is our souls
Though we stumble
Weak with merit
We're blessed enough to grow
Come back
I want to say I'm sorry
Atone for I know
Peace is watching
Gently giving
The harmony of her glow

## All is Stress

All is stress
        don't sleep good tonight
        cupboards dry bare honey
        hungry children cry
        so take a little Prozac
        leave in ganga seed
        mix it up and smoke it, darling
        let it chill out your needs

All is stress mummy
        alone you fight
        cuts and bills in your pocket
        income is tight
        so take a precious tenner honey
        give it to the man
        drown your pickney's needs now darling
        in the heart of oppression
        could you
        take up education
        could you
        look to your vocation
        could you
        love yourself please cos
        womb holds next future mamma
        make sure it stays clean
        single mummy, single mummy cos
        girl you've got to love yourself
        you're feeling stressed out
        girl you've got to teach yourself
        the power to shout out
When,
        all is stress, all is stress
        single mummy

## Depression

Distant but distinct
Senses perceive it's moving in
Thicker as it rolls, faster
Dulling senses
Piercing paranoia
Mindless of reason, it
Destroys intellect, as
All from within it
Blooms fatally
  shaking its aura
Swimming in the odour
Of its hard heart
Its cold breath
Illuminated by suicidal flirtations
It calls you
  by your name

# Pregnant Child

Child-Women thoughts, clashing like a carnival
                in my head
Hopes, lies, dreams, surfing; as the living dead
Deep in the fibres of my African being
The next generation, but where is my healing ?

Born in the trial, in one's young life
Passing of sins, like the vows to a wife
Yearning the bonds of birth and sacrifice
                        that mother pass to child
                            as he enter his life

Drowned in the senses of my unborn being
Rocked to the core, by it's primal beatings
Where is my parent, the parent in me
What is this fate, this identity
How do you give?
When you cannot receive
How do I love myself
To set this child free?

## How Great Thou Art

*to Joseph Samuel, and Olivia Grace*

There's not a precious twinge, of light space
When I don't know my place
I'm your mother
Do you know you make my cup flow
I'm your mother
You're the fruit from my bow
I love you, beings
How great thou art
From now to eternity
Nothing
Can separate our souls
You to me
And you can always fly free
Fly free
You can always fly free
I'm your mother
My precious daughter
Love your scent
Seek everything
You need to be
I'll be your mother, my son
'til the cows come home
I'm your mother
When you've gone, left home
I'll be your mother
When you're all alone
Just remember the passion in me
Walk tall
Be happy

## *Too Many Times*

Too many times
She has cried
Hot scalding tears
That washed her blind
Tears of self pity
For the bed she had made
Their daddy can't be bothered
That is her shame

A taste of disbelief
Clouds her veins
The gift of him
Grows through them both
How can he create love
Then let it go

Too many times
She had cried
As a child
Hot scalding tears
Washed her eyes
Cried for the family
She knew not about
A bitter uncertainty
In a world of self doubt
Too many lies
Too many tries
And now a parent
Tears of self pity
For the bed
She has made
Their daddy can't be bothered
He's got his father to blame

And they've got your eyes
And they've got your smile
And when they cry
It's the child you left behind

Too many times
A woman will cry
When the father
Leaves the kids behind
Oh they had argued
She was a bitch
Too bad to be true
But what did the pickneys
Do to you?

And they've got your eyes
And they've got your smile
And when they cry
It's the child you left behind
And when they cry
It's the child you left behind

Too many times...

# The Woman Inside

Sat on the side of an unmade bed
Duvet rumpled
Staring into a void
Wondering where she'd gone wrong
The cracks, strain
Pressure in her head
Were never in the childhood game
Playing women
Lipstick, fags, high-heeled sophistication
Of a well-sought dame

The woman inside, is crying hard
Feels like she's choking on her heart
Out of her mouth will soon come misery
Spluttering, retching, emotion

Yet her features beautifully remain calm

She's got the quietness of danger
She's ready to pounce
Scorched and scorned
Her pride had been trampled
Her strength had been crushed
For she had forgotten her role
      To do as she's told

## *Peacock*

Who is the peacock?
You or he?
Man and woman
Husband and wife
Only as good as your last grind
Up on top of the social tree
Building walls for no-one to see
Looks are fading how dull you've
Become sold your strength to material wonder
Sullied your looks to plastic crooks
Gave your body
Your essence your love

Sitting stripped put together in finery
Who is the peacock?
You or he
Man and woman
Husband and wife
Alert clever mind clothed in dust
Emotional temperament not safe
To trust
Façade and make-up don't compensate
For your deep messed-up feeling
Your image self-hate
Body wanting, loveless
Piles of comfort skin
Your lives in vain
Are closing in
Who is the peacock?
You or he?
Only as good as your last grind
Cry then peacock
You're out of time

## Carnival Queen

I travelled to London a true Leeds girl
To visit the Notting Hill Carnival Ball
The music was stomping, the jam was pumping
In the gaiety of the thrall
The colours of Nubian, a beautiful reflection
Against rows of police men wall
Pure grace of the sun
Finally won in its fight with misted morn
And I swayed, felt free
Soaked with energy
My craved black thighs
My woof woof cries
Amidst the horn and the cheer
Whistled teeth and dance hall queens
Full up for my peers
We were united, no cities divided
Socaced in afternoon fun
Oh, colours and beauty all around me
Had heaven really begun
Then I saw a face
Beyond earth's gray gates
His eyes, they held a warriors chance
Out of darkness blinded dazzle
His body gnarled, disabled, lame
Shone with the beauty of his smile
I turned to his chair
Astutely aware an angel
Was looking at me
I felt my sin
As Mary Magdalene
And bowed to kiss his skin
He caught my eyes

And soothed my cries
Baptising me with his grin
His intellect spoke the gift of tongues
Today we are celebrating
So I turned away
Safe for another day
And I joined the dance
I joined the hype of the Notting Hill Carnival Ball
I turned to faces from different places
I'd never met before
I swayed felt free
Soaked with energy
For I had seen the mahogany face
Of a real and proper Lord
The boy child in the chair
Led me where my life
My song has just begun

# 7. Monkey

As my life began again in Leeds, so did my old, hidden insecurities. I had married this man for security and here I was. The first house was a money pit. It was pretty enough as it was just situated off the huge Gledhow Valley woods and was close to Roundhay Park. We had a beautiful garden, the previous occupier must have loved gardening as there was a border of beautiful fragrant flowers that grew in the front. At the back of our house we had two lawns with privet bushes that lined and secured the borders of the house. The privets had been trained to arch over each lawn and the kids and I would see hedgehogs, birds and foxes. Coming from the grey concrete blocks of Ellesmere Port this was a delight. Dawn was beautiful at that house, when the mist and dew were rising, when the earth was warming, as the garden looked mystical and enchanting.

We moved in June, Joseph's fourth birthday was approaching. We had a good hot summer so we'd spend a lot of time in the garden with Joseph and Olivia and all the other children, Shaun, Duan, Safia, Namoi, and Joan's boys, Jayden, Kyle, and Antony. We'd paint and play in the garden and Joseph enjoyed his first birthday there. The house had three bedrooms. The children generally slept with me, Paula and Billy moved into the second room and the last room was a box room. Downstairs we had a through-lounge dining area, the whole of the bottom half of the house was DIY'd in a dark orange gloss, a wood panel job, which I think was meant to reflect a country ranch style barn. Whatever had happened to that interior I don't know, but I knew that the previous owner had been a far better gardener than decorator. The wood on the walls had not been smoothed so we often got splinters. This person loved wood so much they had even extended the ranch theme to the front of the house, and the entrance, and the porch.

That first summer the house felt like a haven, it was a good hot summer and we seemed able to settle. Then the winter came.

There was no central heating in the house, we had one gas fire and one hob. The house felt cold and draughty. The dark nights and the burnt orange wood panel gave the house a spooked, lonely feel. Paula, myself and Bill felt like there was something sinister about the house. One night I awoke in a cold sweat, I had a nightmare where I'd dreamt someone was in the spare room. It was a man with yellow-white skin and hair and piercing blue but bloodshot eyes, it looked like a zombie, it screamed bad omen. Billy agreed and said he was having weird dreams too. As Paula was my best friend and Bill had been her boyfriend for along time, he naturally became my best friend and confidant. Billy is a Jamaican man, born in Jamaica and travelled to England as a young boy. He is six feet tall, has the looks of a Nubian guard and is built like an athlete. He is a good friend and we share in a lot of good and bad times. Billy is a great communicator and has immense knowledge, he has a string of qualifications to his name and is happiest when writing his lyrics or playing with the kids. He has a sensitive and superstitious side and would delight us with his talk of Jamaica, its Duppies and his mother who had the gift of tongue. Billy believed in ghosts and Duppies, so shared my suspicions.

\*\*\*

It turned cold like the season. I had no idea how to stop the spiralling bills. The electricity bill had come in and I nearly died when I saw how much it was. Steven had stopped paying money and I was on income support. Steven paid well to start with, guilt money, but after six months he stopped. Gas and electricity token meters were installed. I was living in blind panic. I had diarrhoea every day for the first year. My weight began falling and I started having panic attacks every time I saw somebody at the door who I thought wanted money. The only thing I looked forward to was blocking it out.

I felt like a crap mother and was suicidal. Although, I never actually tried it, I found the prospect of escaping for good exhilarating. General and my people kept a close eye on me. He reintroduced me back into the community of his friends. I met up with Miriam and Valerie, two of his women friends, and they were my rock.

Valerie is a solid woman, she is as you find her and does not ever play mind games. She is trustworthy and an attractive person. Her children, especially her eldest daughter who is at college, reflect the beauty and work she has single-handedly put into them over the years.

Miriam is a best friend. I'd admired her as a young teenager and the thought that she wanted to be my friend was very empowering. Miriam had just come out of a hellish abusive relationship and we clung to each other. We both were extremely weak from the abuse and both had very complex relationships with our mothers. Miriam is of dual heritage. She is Asian and English, she is a very beautiful woman and General named her 'The Holy Mother Miriam,' that suited her spirit.

I was in pretty bad shape emotionally, Miriam was also healing after a devastating and violent relationship. She had survived and taught me the basics of managing and surviving alone, something that I had never really thought about or done until this point. We laughed through our pain and talked in depth to each other how we were feeling and how it effected us. She was able to see what I saw and I was able to see her hurt. Miriam's children, Safia and Naiomi, were all about the same age as Joe and Olivia, only Safia was the oldest. We all grew close and I share a deep sisterly, relationship with Miriam and unconditional love.

\*\*\*

After about six months I started dating. The kids used to stay over at their father's at weekends and holidays, so my time became my own again. I was looking for romance and easy distraction, sex and the pursuit of sex became the way to relieve it. I saw how man did things, so did the same, had some of what I wanted, when I wanted and tried to be discreet. Through the study of self I realise that I have never held a healthy opinion of myself. After my marriage this respect manifested into deep self-hate which I believe leads to all areas of self. I was scared and felt not in control, it birthed in bouts of wild behaviour, if triggered or depressed. I'd disrespect myself first in self. I hated the way I looked, talked and walked. I even hated the way I smelt, I had no concept of loving thyself. I had spent years moving from one home to another, from one culture to another, from one barrier to a block of hard-walled emotions. I had no kin or sameness. I felt inadequate because of that for my children. I could not compare myself with anyone, my earlier life lessons taught me that I was unwanted, always an outsider, a freak. My later ones seemed to teach me that I was worth nothing and that life was for living in the high, away from the madness of frustration, helplessness, anger and pain. I lived a life through other people's eyes and lost myself in the perception that I was a failure. I had a failed marriage, a failed motherhood, for I couldn't be the mother I wanted to be, and again felt like a labelled statistic. The men that I bedded gave me physical love for a night, a few weeks or until they became bored, too close - and sometimes vice versa. I would close my eyes, smell and feel them, pretend that they loved me, pretend they were Mr Right. I always tried to make sure they liked me more than I liked them, it was food for my ego.

I had had two babies, my body was out of shape, tired and stretched. I felt more like a 35 year old than a 25 year old. I had begun to doubt everything I said. I was not confident in my speech, myself, my views, everybody was right, I was wrong.

Strong is a funny word, I used to think strong was to go it alone; face each miserable, penny-pinching day with a bright smile and more than a couple of brandies. I know now that strength is asking for help, for calling in your own special rewards, putting

God first, yourself second, humanity third. It's only in God you feel the sense of who you are and what you are here to do.

\*\*\*

I was working at Harvey's. Harvey's is a wine bar in Leeds and before I left Leeds to go to Switzerland, Harvey's had been the most popular 'in' bar to go to. It played all kinds of music, had a racing car green interior and thick mahogany wood. It was classy in design, different from the other bars in Leeds. It was the first of the first for good food, good music, good surroundings and good looking people. A Scottish guy called Willie was my manager, we got on well. He had a fantastic sense of humour and was a fair boss, we all worked hard for him. There was a fantastic working spirit in Harvey's, everybody got on and it showed. I would perform, smile and dance behind the bar and found the knack of extorting large tips out of people. Soon the other staff complained so I initiated a competition with my work colleagues to find out who could reach the highest amount in tips. Willie loved it as we all began serving, smiling and working much quicker in order to secure fat tips. I used to call out, 'ching ching' when I was given extra money, soon the whole staff did it and the punters seemed to enjoy it. I could go home with an extra £15 in my pocket after sharing out the money with the others. I was out of the house three times a week, Paula would generally look after Joesph and Olivia if they were not with their father or visiting family. Paula enabled me to work, I was able not to worry about the children, at times she seemed like the mother to us all. Billy included.

I worked in Harvey's for about a year, then the brewery who owned it decided to refurbish. After seeing how they stripped away the classic interior, replacing it with an eighties turquoise chequered wallpaper, replacing the mahogany with large, gaudy borders, and after seeing the matching turquoise polyester uniforms, I decided it was maybe time to move on. I remember seeing an advert in the *Yorkshire Evening Post*, 'Attractive and young males and females required for bar work, experience essential, £5 per hour.' This was a lot of money considering I only made just under £3 an hour at Harvey's. This was less hours, more relaxed and tried to have a glamorous feel. It was an American-style bar and the new owner wanted to be flashy. The bar was called Charlie Parker's and was inside the Corn Exchange in the centre of Leeds. I had had good training from Willie and found enormous job satisfaction in working behind the bars. I met a lot of really good friends, Samantha being one of them. I'd met her when she'd first joined Harvey's, I'd been there for a while and was Willie's favourite. Everybody seemed to be whispering behind their faces, when Sandra and Clem, two of my colleagues overheard and demanded what the gossip was. 'Oh,' said Jackie, another work mate, 'it's just that Michelle's got competition.' We did not understand what they were talking about and I was annoyed at their bitchiness until we saw Samantha. Samantha is dark-skinned and fine-boned, her family have Arawk and Indian blood. She has long, silky, jet-black hair and looks like she has been kissed by God. Her grace and form is that of a jaguar, she is a close to perfect in my perception of visual beauty. She is Jamaican, born in England. Her mother has mothered me in troubled times. Samantha had what I'd always wanted, a doting mother, and a strong-rooted black family. She was a lot younger than me but was welcomed into the community of my friends. We all saw great things for her.

We had some good times and at times she felt like a sister, I managed to get her a job in Charlie Parker's and, for six months at least, everything was okay. Samantha then began seeing a man, I had previously had a brief fling with his brother. Deeds express far more than fragile and large egos ever can. This man was manipulating Samantha. I, at, first couldn't believe it as I thought we had put so much groundwork into her. We tried to teach her strut. She was a debutante and she had to use her power over men and not be used by them. Samantha once came running to us and said this man had roughed her up and she was excited by this. She got a buzz because he was dangerous and exciting. We said that he was dangerous and therefore she should stay away from him. When her man asked me to sleep with him in front of Samantha, things came to a head. I was very confused, as I didn't know then not to walk into other people's madness and it hurt me.

\* \* \*

It was the week after Christmas 1995, Joseph and Olivia had gone to their dad to see their family. Paula, Samantha and myself were in town. We decided to go into Charlie Parker's for drinks, as we were in the Corn Exchange. Samantha's man was there, I hadn't seen him since the last incident and had purposely stayed away from Samantha when she was around him. We, Paula and myself, were enjoying a good drink and laugh and were attracting good natured attention, we paid no mind to Samantha as she was talking to him. He called me over, at first I refused, but he was good natured and my drunk spirit was defenceless. He asked why I was not talking to him, I said it was because he was a good businessman but a lousy fuckery friend. He did not like this, so he high-kicked me to the concrete floor. I sprung up and asked him what would his mother think of him beating me up. I had known his beautiful mother and been respected by her. The truth hurt him and the fight began. Paula jumped from nowhere in front of me and we were on the receiving end of his practised karate kicks.

Nobody broke it up and afterwards I was livid and drunk. This man was not going to get away this. Paula and I bought another round of drinks, to calm ourselves. Samantha walked up and kissed him. I was in hell and I knew it. My sense of madness seemed real as life just seemed fucked up. Here I was walking out of a marriage for a beating, thinking I'd got away, when another man who I had no love connection with gave me a beating anyway.

Annie and Dominic were brilliant. Dominic had this thug-dog arrested immediately but found he was in the cells anyway, for beating up his baby mother. Annie explained to me that I had depression, and it could be sorted if I took myself to the doctor's. They were loving and gentle with me and I appreciated their concern. I took Prozac for a couple of months and moved with the help of the Citizens Advice Bureau, out of the moneypit house and towards a fresh beginning. I was determined to survive, and my sense of self was always appreciated and rewarded by my close friends. I had started to write poetry again, but kept it to myself. My need to look for myself, in the form of my father, resumed and my house on 69 Scot Hall Road began to take life. I was living on my income support and managing, my friends remained close and helpful. I thought everything was going smoothly and forgave Samantha, in order, I thought, to move on.

\* \* \*

Samantha and I were out one night, in town, we had had a good night and we had been at Uropa, a really sad club with bad music, but one that you can have a good laugh in. We had seen the thug-dog in the club and avoided him. Samantha had by this time been stung by him in more than a few ways and a mutual friend of ours, Claire, had taken over her punchbag position. We left the club and were offered a lift home by a friend, he was only going part the way, so we agreed to get a taxi, or walk from there. The Hayfield was still open, so we went in to buy a drink and phone a taxi. The thug-dog followed us in and was trying to get our attention by slagging us. I walked over to Samantha and said something, I can't remember, the next thing I was high-kicked to the dance floor, in the middle of the Hayfield; my pub, the pub in which my birth parents had met. I was thrown out, he followed, there was a massive crowd around us. They gathered round while he beat me up, again. I was getting badly hurt, my sense of survival turned my spirit started talking, I was screaming at the faces, at him, blindly, but clearly, 'You can kick my body but you can't kill my spirit,' and 'Bum, bye bye, in thug-dog's head, I'm gonna get some man, to shoot you dead.' I mentioned a friend's name and it did not help. The thug-dog after kicking me up, went to the police station where he informed them that I had been harassing him, he got his brother and his friend to beat me up, and continue beating me while he was talking to the police. Samantha acted bravely but she was no match for three men. The police were cold and crap, they had a patronising air. They did nothing, even though I had photographs and reports from my first attack at the same police station. At this point I lost all respect for authority and anything governmental. To me, this incident was blatantly racist, this was no domestic attack, this was assault. You can bet that if this had been a white woman attacked by a Black man, he would have been in the cells that very same night. Get him first, ask questions later.

Gone were the Marley days, we were living in the shadow of Thatcher and her materialistic Gods. The local Tory party had ruled over the Chapeltown community for years. This community that had naturally thrived with street dancing, sounds, dance groups, singing groups, youth groups and Carnivals, was suddenly disbanded to make way for the new incarnation of a council funded community. A propaganda war was launched by the *Evening Post* and people began to feed off the lies and stereotypes. I could see strong people falling. People I'd known for years were overdosing, entering mental hospitals, suffering and selling class A substances. It was 1997 and I felt the rage of my community, I shared the rage of my community. The system and its game, its hype had let me down, as a woman and as mother, and although I was mostly always dry, sometimes I felt I needed to get a little high.

*Years of bottled pain, years of sorting the bullshit and the blame*
*Years of cold, rainy, winter, days*
*Years of electricity tokens*
*Years of negativity rides*
*Too many years of abusing myself inside*
*So I got high*
*I took the drugs because I chose to*
*Fighting the escapism and running from the truth*
*Years of raves and jungle bliss*
*Years of good*
*Years of bad*
*Tripping on the talking not all I had*
*Suddenly, ducked, some times dive*
*Now to find my truth inside*
*It comes in a spiritual climb*
*Learning of truth with forgiveness in mind*
*Years of two faced lies*
*MotherGod, my light*
*She helped me rise.*

Because I am Catholic born and raised, I know I carry a lot of their guilt. Sexual guilt, marriage guilt, weakness guilt, sin guilt and jealousy guilt. It transformed me from conscious and confident to shallow and insecure; not about others but about myself. On hearing of the events, Paula Fitzmaurice, who was chosen by me, Mum and Dad to be my godmother, vocalised the shocked angry response I was looking for. She told me I was a survivor. I knew it but needed someone to tell me, someone I believed in. Even though she had her own life, Paula, my friend, was always there. She kept telling me one day she wasn't going to be around, I believed her. Miriam stood firm for me and we would laugh and laugh, in pain, in poverty, in friendship. We relived our fears to one another, empowering and learning to be there for each other's children. Miriam, like all my close friends, is spiritual and intelligent. Miriam introduced me to a man called

Louis Barker. Louis owned and ran a multicultural bookshop, specialising in Afro, Black and Asian literature. I worked for him voluntarily and his kindness and his spirit was empowering and comforting. I loved working at various events, it gave me back a grain of my old self respect. I was surrounded by literature and history, Black African and American, classics of all titles were sold and, as I devoured the books, my spirit began its healing process.

I took a complete step back from the manic life served by walking in other people's madness. I began to sort and assess. I stopped holding everyone else responsible and started holding myself accountable. I recaptured my love of learning and began to take pride in my own small accomplishments. I got a buzz from selling books I knew had helped me, my poetry began to breathe again and I stopped running and turned around to face my fears.

## Extract From Adoption Files

**11.2.72** Vacancy at Mill Green Close was discussed at allocation meeting for Michelle.

**14.2.71** Miss Egan[1] is thrilled to be having Michelle at Mill Green. All the other children are excited about meeting her.

**16.2.71** Took Michelle for day to Mill Green. Michelle responded well to the older children and played happily all day.

**3.3.72** Michelle booked in for minor operation on her ear. Michelle seems more confident in her movements but is still not walking yet. She shows a pleasing response to affection.

**24.3.72** Transferred Michelle to Mill Green. She was tearful at leaving the nursery but appeared content once established in the home. Michelle received a genuine warm welcome from the Housemother and other children.

**25.4.72** Visited Michelle. She appears to have settled remarkably well. Miss Egan has made arrangements for her to be baptised at the local RC church. Michelle loves to play out in the garden and can demonstrate quite a temper when she is told to come in.

**15.6.72** Michelle is making excellent progress and is now running around, and at times being quite naughty. Still only speaks odd words but is developing gradually. Michelle is a happy little child and responds to encouragement.

**21.8.72** Mrs Moran called and wanted to have the baby home for a few days. She has been in the psychiatric unit for six weeks and is home on leave. I explained it would not be possible. She asked if they could visit. I said I would arrange this. She asked if they could go on a Wednesday as that was when Mr Clarke got his Giro and they wanted to buy her a present.

**23.8.72** Visited Michelle who had been delighted with her holiday to the seaside and was at home in her toddler's bathing pool. Miss Egan says Michelle is absolutely no trouble and is happy in the company of other children. No sign of Mrs Moran when I left.

**24.8.72** Mrs Moran is back in hospital having slashed her arms the previous day.

[1] Aunty Carmel

## Affirmation

I am a survivor
I affirm my choice in my chosen journey
I am a child of God
I am proud to be and know where to start
I am a passion-filled
Loving mother to my children
I am a kind, happy, silly aunt to many children
I am blessed
I forgive myself in the clarity of God
I call on my mother ancestors
I call on all my father ancestors
I call all the wisdom from God holy spirit
I call on all the peace from the heavens
I am whole

# *Monkey*

She took a sip of brandy
Her monkey awoke
It pranced off her back
Liquid slid down her throat

She excites the monkey
He's going to see her slump
Oh to watch her weakness
He loves to see her drunk

It's hard to take
Hard to watch the show
It's hard to watch
Her monkey glow
It's hard to take

In the blare of the next morning
She'd think you were the fool
Think that you were lying
To protect who?

Cigarettes and coffee
Nicotine and cocaine
Heroin and crack
Monkey loves it the same
When you see your monkey
Remember it's name
Let it go, free it
Forgive it your shame

It's hard to take
Hard to watch the show
It's hard to watch
As her monkey glows
It's hard to take

In the blare of the next morning, girl
She'd think you were the fool
Think that you were lying
To protect who?

It's hard to take
Watch her go
It's hard to watch
Her one-woman show
It's hard to watch

## *Baby*

And it's in the way you feel,
     baby
That it's craving to be alright

And it's what you don't say,
     baby
That makes me wake at night

And it's 'cos you can leave me,
     baby
That claws me close to you

Falling into the pit,
     baby
What's a woman to do?

And I knew all the rules,
     baby
When I held you tight

And I know you play it hard,
     baby
When you rocked me high

Could not get enough,
     baby
Of your dark-skinned smile

Well some friends are lovers,
     baby
But I cannot give you lie

When you deep inside,
     baby
Then you feel all mine

# Paranoid Pain

We got ya, we got ya
The hyenas seem to cry
And now you're not going anywhere
Cos you're too, too dry

They're starin' at me
They're gonna kick me down
They wanna see me trip
They wanna see me frown

I walk high and tall
Cos when I'm not pissed I don't fall
And I walk like the African sisters before
Black and proud as dignity is my shroud

Not 'fraid of the beating and the degradation
Of Black fighting Black
After slavery done

I'm tired of being strong
But I have to hold on
To the paranoid pain
'Cos it might happen again

We got ya, we got ya
The hyenas seem to cry
But they're not goin' anywhere
'Cos they're too, too dry

## *Take Time*

To all the boys to man on the line
With all your style, your sting, your shine
       you pretty Black boys
       you waste my time
You look like sometin' me wanna eat
Lyrics you talk are fraud but sweet
       hidden talents discarded and weak
       is that what your mama worked so hard for?
         and what did you really
            wanna be
         a fireman, a lecturer, a Gee
            stop
         England is your reality
         quit flirting with American fantasy
            caw
         is coming like a tidal wave
         to crash us down to the floor
While you sell your crack
Like sweet and candy
         our destruction is in store

## *Vampire*

I'm the vampire of the night
Drink your taste
Till you're mine
Lead you round
With the games I'll play
      I'll play on your soul
           That you gave away

I'm the vampire of the night
You're more than just my valentine
Bite your neck
Swallow your life
Leave you searching
      for the love you'll not find

I don't know how to love,
So I'll take that from you
Kinder you are
More you'll lose
Watch yourself when you come close to me
I'm addictive sensuality

## Spanish Junkie

Every night she stands alone
Beauty lighting the pavement stone
Hung to waste her slight stoned smile
Sold her body to flee her mind
Smacked brown nasty
She injects her veins
Time to walk the streets again

Oh, it feels so nice to be high
Sold her body to flee her mind
Fire and brimstone, beauty, rage
Spanish junkie, flamenco grace

When I pass her though
As I walk on by
I show her my smile
For a little while
For in the blind of sunlight
The blink of an eye
Shadow of the junkie
Turns into your child

Oh, it feels so nice to be high
Sold her body to flee her mind
Fire and brimstone, beauty, rage
Spanish junkie, flamenco grace

And for just another second
Another moment, another high
A time when her mind was clean and dry
A second in which her tongue was freed
And her laugh, her laugh was all it should mean
Ha ha ha, can you help her

Oh, it feels so nice to be high
Sold her body to flee her mind
Fire and brimstone, beauty, rage
Spanish junkie, flamenco grace

And she's
She's dancing slow senorita
Can you feel her mind
She's dancing
Can you see her dancing?
She's dancing
On the dragon
her knees clamped
For the ride
the rhythm rougher than reality
She's on the wrong side
Can you help her?

Oh, it feels so nice to be high
Sold her body to flee her mind
Fire and brimstone, beauty, rage
Spanish junkie, flamenco grace

Dancing
Aimlessly
Gleefully
Lost to all
Locked to street
Punter
Dealer
Pusher
The appalled
Walk past me
Watch me fall

You see
It don't seem no sacrifice
Between the needle
Or the fist in the eye
That's why she needs
So high
Needs to leave it
All behind
And can you help her?
Or can you
Watch her fall?

Every night
She walks alone
And as I pass her by
I remember
Her spirit
Herself denied
One day
She'll fly
Through the eye of the needle
To God's sunlight

## My Story

I feel so sad
Like a pain, like a wound
That I never had
It's hard to explain
Maddening, destructive
Abuse
Rises again
It rises again

Alcohol does me bad
Like a drug, in my body
That I never had
It's hard to explain
You see the liquor
The liquor
Stills my pain
Stills my brain

Tell me do you think I'm mad
Or just a human with a story
Everyone has?
It's hard to explain
If you took this path
You'd feel the same
Feel the same

And I know just what it is
Just a journey in life
'Til death's final kiss
It's hard to explain
But I don't think life
Will ever be the same
Look the same
Taste the same

## Suburbia Hype

Wild in form
Clumsy in fall
Laughter of a mating call
Here I am now
Hunter and hide
Begging forgiveness
In suburbia hype
Reasons I cannot explore
Don't want to hold back no more

Bitten the apple
Come off in the hype
Madness in madness
I'm losing my mind
In suburbia hype
Reasons I cannot explore
Don't want to hold back no more

Bitten the apple
Come off in the high
Pre-occupational hazard
In I'm losing my mind
Take my hand the very last time
Leave the ground and the earth behind
Let's fly
Leave suburbia hype behind
Leave suburbia hype

And so you see
I'm begging forgiveness
You see I'm begging forgiveness
Jus' a-begging forgiveness
To the one true light
In suburbia hype

## Cak

He lived by the gun
Died by the gun
Shot for fun
Cracked young son
He lived by his fear
Walked the dark side
His humanity and compassion
Left to one side

He's as famous as a cowboy
For his near-death misses
His yellow Porsche car
Sick sinister disses
His hood rats trigger-happy
Scared of the light
The leader don dead
Nowhere to hide

Born to this society
Cut in two
No fitting no substitute
Laughed and scorned
Through child to man
Took up the crack
With gun in his hand

Eleven shootings in my neighbourhood
Nobody laughing nothing understood
I heard the Grapevine, that he loved
Was loved an' missed
Yet he danced with Satan, and Satan tripped.

# 8. Spirit Journey

I was still working with Lewis in Positive Image and we were asked to work at the Alhambra Theatre in Bradford. It was an African Awareness Day and it was a buzz to see my people here of all different walks. Lemn Sissay was performing that day, I had never heard a British Performance Poet never mind a Black man. He has a presence that surrounds him, he talks his truth and reels his rhyme, nothing like mine, but connecting deep all the same. He was walking on a talking poetry. He was living my dream, I had but dreamt it and knew that my material felt like mine too. I marched up to him afterwards and told him that I was a poet, with some of his experiences and asked if he would look at some of my material. He is a beautiful spirit and agreed enthusiastically. He wrote almost immediately and encouraged me to carry on. He liked my poetry and liked the images. Miriam and myself sat and read the letter over and over. A surge of relief filled me, I felt that at last I had confirmation, I could be a poet, this was something I knew I could work at for the rest of my life. It was mine, belonged to me, I had never had that feeling about my destiny before. My choice of vocation felt real, was sealed .

My depression lifted and I began to pour my energies into performing and writing my poetry. My words started to make sense with people, as it seemed when I was 13. I started once again to feel worthy of communicating. Most of my first gigs were in Chapeltown, and my community listened and accepted my chosen profession. I joined DemDaya, a Black theatre group. I began to meet people who walked, talked and lived through creativity. Most of DemDaya had been in the business of performing arts and held good grace. I was fortunate to be among these friends because they each held valuable lessons and insights for me. I will always appreciate the space that they gave me in my new found self. I recall my memories and can capture Ayo's smile, Chester's warmth, Wesley's sensitivity, Glynis's shy sharp mind, J C's gaiety, Freddy's lesson's on ego and self and

Joe's enormous sense of humanity, his personal wealth. I can always delight when I see new talent because of my training and teaching from DemDaya and Miriam. Joe Willams took time to support my progress. They taught me to share and see as a team. I was hungry for everything. I felt at peace with myself in a new adult way. I was a survivor, I did not know how to tackle all of my inner fears so chose to forgive everyone and everything. It was too long, too painful and too demanding for me to forgive myself for the person I was but I felt that if I stopped blaming and hating others for my misfortunes and concentrated on being a good mum while working at my poetry I could then keep captured this peace that I felt. Through my poetry I was able to speak of my pain and of the madness I saw around me without being beaten up. When performing my poetry I was able to shake off the rage and anger and turn it into energy. My spirit felt like my instrument, I felt highly motivated and full of enthusiasm. I had to find the questions so that I could get back to the answers. I felt that my children and myself could not look forward to anything better if I did not face my fears.

\*\*\*

Miriam, Martin, Lewis and myself had organised a huge show in the Quarry Theatre at the West Yorkshire Playhouse. The show was to raise money for Kush and other community, grass roots projects and to promote awareness and achievement in education for Black and Asian children. I was full up with ambition and drive. I wanted to show people, councils, arts boards, education boards that two unemployed, single mums could pack out the Quarry with the faith from Garfield Allen, Lemn Sissay, David Hamilton, Inder Goldfinger, Lewis and Martin not to mention the true winners of the night, the children, and the Leeds Black Elders, with the work from all the untold I forget to mention. We wanted to show how little the council were doing, we succeeded.

Garfield Allen was the Black arts coordinator at the Playhouse. I remember our first meeting with him. I was nervous, my hands were sweaty and clammy, I was also ambitious, I wanted the Quarry Theatre as it was the largest and seated over four hundred people. Miriam was cool, witty and collected. We'd practised hard in front of each other, our grace manner and pose, for what we were asking was a gamble. We bombarded and astounded Garfield. I remember Miriam ending our presentation and proposal with, 'So, Garfield, what can you do for us?' From that moment Garfield trusted, put his faith in, backed us and protected us from our critics. Miriam and myself secured £250 from Leeds City Council as we were in the 'Year of Anti-racism,' to help towards the show. Although we worked hard writing and asking for sponsors nothing else materialised. Garfield matched our money and hired Ishmal Thomas from the Real McCoy, to host the show. One of my friends, Carlton, was in his finals of a photography degree and gave his time and creativity willingly, Miriam and myself were in a working dream.

That night we had a host of different groups from the Black communities in Leeds. We then had professional Black performers, poets, dancers and comedians. We wanted to mix professional artists with local talent as it acted as inspiration and role modelling. We hoped to show all sections and ages of the Black community coming together to vocalise and visualise their talent and creativity. I performed my piece with DemDaya. Our whole piece was about finding self and the light through our experiences. Lemn Sissay had graciously said that he would perform his poetry. David Hamilton from RJC dance group said that he would perform a dance piece which was really good of him because he was touring abroad. We had the Black elders, the prominent elders of our community, the Windrush peoples and the war veterans performing two drama improvisations, it went down beautifully. The audience, packed full of family and community, roared their appreciation for the smooth, strong, old-timers. What started as a dream and perception on my part turned into a hard reality.

At first I had come to Miriam and Lewis with the idea as it became evident to me as a poet that unless I staged my own shows I would not become known or be able to make enough contacts. Being a single mum, I had to arrange babysitters and I had a burning desire to make my poetry work. If I waited to be asked, I felt like I would miss out and yet I realised that I could never get to my dreams alone, they had to be shared to become real. I think for Miriam it enabled her to put her views and debate into action, she has been in education for the past fifteen years, she worked in various trained disciplines and is a front line community leader on Black awareness and education. What Miriam can instil and give to people is truly what describes her character, she's the only person I know in Chapeltown who the feared, the forgotten and written-off will seek guidance from. She carries trust. I can equate her with the Holy Mother Miriam. General named her wisely. I have seen the whole world in her kitchen, I have seen how she flourishes belief into people, instilling encouragement, and listening.

Miriam asked local hip hop artists to perform. There was Kani and LP and DJ X then she introduced them to Inder Goldfinger. Inder Goldfinger is an Asian musician, a local Leeds boy well-known and liked in the community. He is an international musician playing with the likes of Ian Brown and the Stone Roses. Inder is a humble, twinkley man, he loves his tracksuits, loves his family and loves his God. He inspired and put a lot of his skills into the show.

The night of the show came about with relief and gladness, it had been a long and difficult learning curve. It's then that I learnt to make a dream reality, it took faith and hard work. It was not the most organised of shows, I, having to perform and organise, went into a complete emotional happy state when the front of house called backstage to us to tell us that the show was completely sold out. Everybody relaxed and there was drinking and smoking backstage, it was like carnival. I stood there thinking that this was it, everybody was helping everybody, we had people offering their services in make-up, wardrobe and hair. It was a joyful extravaganza. People from Chapeltown, Harehills and surrounding areas were together, giving their all and having a damn good night. I was high on vibes and achievement, we sold out. I can still taste the feeling. Miriam and I were ecstatic, we had done it. It ran two hours over time due to the fact Miriam and myself had never done this before. The Playhouse staff were patient and good-willed, but we had done it and covered all costs. We had never told people that it was going to be the best staged variety show they'd ever seen, we wanted to show that the community was out there and talented.

*** 

My spirit healing, my confidence returning, I organised myself in my new life, I took control of my body, of my thoughts, of my sexuality. I took control of my weakness, humbled myself to God, reconfirmed and had reconfirmation of MotherGod. I began to see light in my poetry. Marylin and Paula had backed me from the age of thirteen, Miriam became my agent and nurtured and boosted my self-confidence.

After the Kush event Miriam worked hard for me as my agent. She had many talented people on her books. First of all she introduced me to James Berry who had read my poetry and said he was interested in meeting me. At the meeting he told me that my poetry wasn't really poetry, just affirmation. He told me that unless I wanted to be another community poet, then I'd have to go to workshops and study. I walked away from that meeting in York feeling defiant and determined to keep my poetry real. At the end of the day, I did not need a literature prize to make people think.

Miriam then booked me a gig with Benjamin Zephaniah on a Leeds City Leisure project organised by Steve Byfield. I was wildly excited at the prospect, however my friend Mary's sister had just won a trip to South Africa for two weeks. I was invited along. I had to decide between Benjamin and Africa. I chose Benjamin. On the day of the performance I was cool, calm and collected. I had given up too much not to be. I had all my titles written on my hands and was over-rehearsed. I kept thinking I was going to forget my lines. Onyeka stood up first, he is a young, strong, male writer, his first novel was called *Waiting to Explode*. It described the many different kinds of Black experience using different characters. While he was talking about the book he mentioned a character of mixed race adopted into a white family. This was my cue. I had spoken to Benjamin earlier and implored him to listen to my poetry. I could see him watching as I stood up. I first welcomed my parents and the audience seemed warmed. As I was the only female performer I seized the opportunity and became womanly and warm. My first poem was *Girls*, the audience loved it. The second poem was *Windrush* for the elders who had come all the way into town to support me. They loved it. *One Forgotten Princess* had people crying. I finished with *MotherGod*. The audience didn't respond, they sat there in silence. They forgot to announce Benjamin, so he in a good-mannered way broke the silence and introduced himself. From that day Benjamin, as Lemn, has been a massive support.

I had always loved to sing but always held the conception that my voice was weird, when my poetry deepened so did my singing. I began to sing my poetry, not all of it, but bits that I felt needed that expression. I was extremely unconfident about my singing ability but was determined to find someone and play poetry and sound in any way it felt like it should come out.

* * *

It was Samantha who first heard of Aerron Perry through her hairdresser, Shaun Udo. Aerron was not from Chapeltown and we knew nothing about each other before we met. Aerron lived in Holbeck, which is the opposite side of town from Chapeltown.

It has always been stereotyped, I have certainly always stereotyped it as a National Front area, heart of Leeds United, Elland Road. A no-go area for me in my skin. I wasn't sure of what to expect when we knocked at his house. His partner Mark opened the door and was polite and charming. I was taken aback by their front room, which was painted artfully in burnt orange and their eye for design, arranging, collecting and nesting, I'd heard men could be house-proud but had never met or seen any evidence before. Aerron had set up his first studio in the basement. There was barely enough room to fit three people and that added to the groovy feel. I was elated and excited as I heard Aerron talk of his passion for making music because it matched my ambition to take poetry as far as I could and run with it. I felt his music and loved it. My words and poems fizzed open, we were aware of what we were doing as our vibes were so compatible with each others. It fit like a glove.

My first impressions of Aerron were a slim, tall man with a Dirk Bogard aura, intense yet kind, friendly and gentle. Aerron, I think, was born knowing his destiny and is happy in spirit and self. It showed and I was ready to have some of that clarity for myself. Both me and Aerron have come from large families and have lots of brothers and sisters, that's what makes us alike in many ways. This friendship I have with Aerron is a lifetime blessing whether we work together or not. I don't see us being different too much in spirit, it is our packaging and differing sexuality that makes us seem different. We wrote about 15 songs in the first three weeks. Poems that I had not used for a while began to appear as drumbeats, tones, creations of Aerron's new music, we couldn't believe how easy we found it, creating a song. Aerron is a true friend, I would like to think we had a great respect for each other. I have never had a friendship with so many qualities as this one has. Aerron is of Welsh and Irish descent born in England, 31, funny, quiet, determined, highly creative and lives with his partner and spiritual guide, Mark. These are two men who know spirit, they know their truth and it holds betterment and perception. Aerron, poetry, music, my song has now begun.

\*\*\*

Just before my twenty-eighth birthday, I went for a routine smear test. I was diagnosed with pre-cancerous cells and was told I would have to have an operation to remove a large part of my cervix. All my old issues around sexuality, self and guilt, came flooding back. I had not been able to forgive myself, I did not think I could be so scared or feel so lonely, feel so afraid of fear again, but it opened up myself with it.

\*\*\*

I had met a man born on the 18th, this held massive significance to me as I was born on the 18th, as were my children and, later, I found out, my birth mother. I had said to my friends Paula and Miriam that I was not going to see any man, much less love him and date him if he was not born on the 18th. As a child, the 18th of October was my only affirmation that I was born. I was told by clairvoyants that 18 is a strong number, for 1 means the beginning, the first, the start, and 8 is infinity, like DNA. I met Bassy in the Faversham, a student pub in Hyde Park. We started as friends but I was deeply attracted to him and gave him the first few snogs. When he told me a few weeks later that he was born on the 18th I felt that this was a message for union. I felt deeply in love with this strong, stable, intelligent Black man. His family opened their door and shared celebrations and life with myself and my children. Bassy's Momma is a woman of God. She loves her children in their all, each person secure. She stands on her mountain and her children and their kin honour their mother and father.

Bassy is four years younger than myself. He shines so bright, he genuinely holds star quality and at times clasped my hand firmly through many of my journeys back to myself. I give thanks and a blessing to his family and future children as I start to breathe in my own time. Our relationship has now ended. Bassy is to walk this part of his journey alone. His future, his creativity and his career need space to grow and finish. He has many hurdles before finishing his multimedia degree. I feel he is going to be a very prominent, important figure in the media, and his ideas on social awareness and activating social responsibility are global, fresh and ground-breaking. When I look at Bassy, to his spirit, I see a great warrior, a great chief. I feel honoured to have love for him, I am proud to be his friend. I am passionately, deeply in love with my children and wanted our love to unify. This meant Bassy taking a more active role in our life, something he was not yet ready to do, yet my children were asking and deserved this. Bassy tried hard to understand where I was coming from and I tried hard to explain. We stopped walking and working together and began talking at each other.

One of Bassy's brothers, Ernest, is a social worker. He is a highly perceptive and sensitive man. He told me once in a conversation that babies and children who were placed in institutions and care homes in their formative years often found relationships difficult as they found the concept of love hard for they did not have unconditional love in their early years to hold up as any kind of measure. This, when said, put all my relations I had had with parents, carers, teachers and boyfriends in a new perspective, one that I hadn't seen before. I came out of this relationship holding the respect, love and peace that I entered the relationship with. I had learnt sometimes to love is to let go, to love is to expect nothing for yourself and greatness for others, for then your rewards will come as huge exciting, developing surprises, always enjoyed like love.

I met my father when I was 27 years old. I had heard so many stories, had so many leads, so many times I had given up. In my search I was told that I had a Jamaican and African father, I was given lots of false names before I found Mitchell Clarke. The need to find my father rather than my mother was my need for affirmation in my Black skin. The previous two years had brought out my survival instincts. After the beating it seemed to me that if I'd had my Black family around then I would have been protected. Also, Bassy came from a very large and loving West Indian family. I began to wonder again who I was like or if I took after anybody. I needed to know my own truth, however bad it was. As a child I would have great fantasies about my birth father. I thought he would be slightly mysterious, an artist. It never once crossed my mind that he wouldn't want to see me.

One day my adoptive father answered a question that I'd been asked by one of the mums at my children's school who wondered if she could trace a nephew. I causally asked my dad and he told me there was an organisation called Catholic Care. I remember feeling shocked, I said he hadn't told me before. He said of course he had; Claire, my sister, had been there earlier that pervious year. I could not remember but knew I'd been told somewhere along the line. Catholic Care ran a children's home and mother and baby unit in Headingley, it's two minutes away from the Scally house and my mum used to work there. I remember feeling surreal as I walked into the building, I knew that something, anything, could come out of this. Maria, a woman from Catholic Care, explained that because I was in care before 1975 my notes were held by the Official Secrets Act and I would have to have two counselling sessions before proceeding. I remember feeling really disillusioned as it seemed or felt like I was still in the systems belly.

Maria is a mixed race woman who had been through the system herself. She took me to a side room and gave me information directly from the files, but for me to view them would be a different procedure. Maria filled me in. I wasn't listening to all that she said as I was hungry for my father. She wasn't allowed to give me his name but she gave me his first name, Mitchell, and his last known address. This was in Chapeltown. There was only two Mitchells in Chapeltown. With this information, I had the wherewithal to find him.

It is very hard to describe the feeling of someone giving you back your self, your story. When I was a child and I would blow the spores off the dandelion I would wish to be able to see my father, just for a picture, something to put in my mind. I was told my birth father had tried to fight and tried to get custody but they wouldn't let him because they were extorting maintenance for his other children. My father's sisters had already taken in five mixed race babies and had no more room when I came.

I looked through the electoral register and in 69 Leopold Street, his last known address, there was a reference to Mitchell Clarke. This had to be him. Bassy tried to bring me to earth the day I found my father, but he did not know where to reach me. He was caring and concerned, I was about to taste my truth at last. The feeling of coming face to face with my father was like seeing fairies because it was such a dream away and now I was in the middle of it. I was really determined to see him so when I found his name in the electoral register I spoke to Maria and told her that I was going to see him. She begged me to wait until after she had phoned him for she didn't want to shock him. She decided to knock on his door as she was worried I might not be able to wait. Fifteen minutes later I was at home, I received a call, it was Maria, my father was asking to see me now, he didn't want to wait.

I was stressing at home, Bassy was trying to calm me, it was like labour all over again but without the pain. It was that intense excitement of knowing you are going to get some answers. My father had lived in Chapeltown since he left Nevis over 40 years ago. He lives 10 minutes away from me and I managed to smoke three cigs in the two minute car journey. When we arrived at his door the third cig had been lit. I was in a panic, what if he didn't like me? What if my hair wasn't right? What was he going to tell me? How would I feel? Suddenly the third cig became as important as my first spliff. Maria knocked on the door and my voice, mind and senses left me, I felt very much like the six year old at the doorstep of a new start. The first thing that struck me was his house, it had a faint smell of garlic and seasoning and was spotlessly clean. I thought to myself, I don't take after him then because my house is constantly messy as I am messy by nature. My father wouldn't let me smoke in the house so I was sent back to the doorstep to finish my cig. My father acted like he had seen me only yesterday and told me that the last time he had had contact with me was when I was five. This shocked me as I had no recollection of this, he said it was good job I'd found him because he was thinking of ringing Cilla Black! He said he knew deep down that I would come looking for him because he loved me. My father then told me I was named after him and if I'd been a boy my name would have been Mitchell. I didn't say much in fact I didn't say anything at all. I just stared, he laughed at me and told me that was the same look I used to give him when I was a baby.

*Silence falls upon me when I looked into his face*
*I loved him then a new born babe*
*I love him now*
*I sat in complete silence staring*
*I could not take my eyes off his face*
*His skin, his build, his eyes, his lips*
*I stared*
*I stared at the way his fingers were shaped like mine*
*That his eyes were almond-shaped like mine*
*My desolation left me*
*My woman exhales*
*I stared at his features*

*Cut like my son from the vine*
*Our silence was warm*
*We agreed in time*
*Silence falls upon me*
*As he spoke my fate released my grace*

My birth father told me my truth. It was not pleasant but it was mine. He told me how he and my mother had had some really good times, how they laughed, how she would get angry and how, in those tempers, he couldn't understand her Irish accent. How they would drink and drink and dance. My father tells me how she would drink every day, and how she was in mental, physical and emotional pain. My mother became poorly, mentally ill somewhere along that line, probably aggravated by her pregnancy and the stress in her past life. My father tells me the story of how she used to scream at me and call me a 'fucking black bitch.' How she used to stand over my cot and rant and curse at me. My father came in once and found her suffocating me. The third time she did this, he beat her up, then carried me to the Social Services on Roundhay Road.

My father forgets her illness and remembers her spirit, he talks of my full-brother who did not have a remembered name. My mother fell pregnant immediately after she had had me, my brother would have been her sixth child. As he remembers he connects me with myself. My mother to the best of my truth, was born in Ballymena, Ireland. Her maiden name was Watson, but she married a man called Moran who was a bully and a drunk. They had three children together and they each received a prison sentence in Ireland for abuse and cruelty to their children. My mother met my father shortly after in Leeds, they met in Chapeltown's waterhole, The Hayfield. There was a four-year relationship in which I was born and my brother died. Their affair reigned between hell and mental fury.

My files indicate that my mother suffered from mental illness, she was said to have self-harmed herself, cutting her arms. She fought alcoholism, and ran to it. My father laughs and calls her a terrorist, she told him once she was going to petrol bomb him. He said he had never run so fast. 'She scared the fucking shit out of me,' he laughs, remembering.

My father recalls the last time he saw her, his neighbour cussed him as he returned from work, 'Why didn't you tell me you were moving? We've been friends all this time…' My father ran into the house; everything, even the carpets, had been taken.

My father will say she was a good looking woman, 'She was a smart woman, your mother, well dressed, a good cook, and she made a good Irish stew.' He tells me she was petite, natural blonde, a real catch. My half-brother Johnny, my father's son, tells me that he was her favourite and would often get taken down the shops to buy sweets. It comforts me when I hear her memories come alive. It makes me feel warm, it makes my spirit feel light.

I used to envy, to the point of bitterness, my Black female friends who had their natural parents around them. They seemed so confident, so cool. My middle-class white accent embarrassed me in my early and late teenage years. It did not go with my face. I tripped and fell and realised I'd been down that road before, with the white girls at school. I could not talk Patios, so did not begin. Until I met my father I was uneasy with my enforced self-ignorance. I am glad at least I had an ear of sense. Imagine if I'd mimicked a friend's Yardie accent, my Nevis father would have told me, 'Wrong island girl.' I was proud of being Black, as the races of the sun were called. I just longed to know my personal history.

I wanted to find my father and I found him, I also found aunties, uncles and cousins. Everyday I walk past a member of my family, each day without recognising it. I had longed for something that is all around me, that I was blind to. It was like having Joseph and then Olivia again, I felt quite free. I was in the transition of lots of fresh bright new changes. I was learning and enjoying being me. I quickly dug myself out of the hole I had made.

***

By 1999 I was on my second operation. I came to the conclusion that I needed, wanted, some other help. I had been to see clairvoyants and I had been introduced to some very spiritual godly people. I needed to understand me and cope with my fear and feelings of dirt and self disgust. I realised that I needed to put my story straight for me in order to walk to womanhood. I wanted to seek clarity in some way I trusted. I had been offered a part in a play, the *Carnival Messiah*, as understudy of 'MotherGod' I was blessed to meet Ella. She is a Shango priestess and she is from Trinidad. I was completely in awe of her sense of self, sense of God, sense of truth. From the heart of Motherland, she cleansed the show, her voice, her direction, a blessing. I remember telling her once that I needed to be directed, I said 'Direct me to direct myself.' She hugged me and told me when I was ready, to call her. I remember how disappointed she was in the huge geographical, mental and emotional displacement of the cast, young and old. I remember telling her she was a rose in the parched deserts of our minds.

Jean 'Binta' Breeze, is a wonderful and beautiful poet. She played 'MotherGod.' I was honoured to learn and work beside her. I was taught invaluable life lessons through Jean 'Binta' Breeze and I strived to learn from them. Jean's greatest gift was her good friend Annette. Geraldine O'Conner wrote and directed the *Carnival Messiah* and I was privileged to see and be part of her 10 year dream as it became her reality. I worked alongside David Hamilton, a professional dancer. I've known him since I was a child because he lodged with my godparents, Paula and Dave. He became the person I went to for advice. I grew a lot during my contract with the *Carnival Messiah*. I had a lot of learning to do, and there seemed many teachers. One of the ladies in the community choir had been through the CIN procedures I can't remember her name because I'm bad for remembering names but I remember her spirit and her smile. We sat and talked for a while. She told me that she'd had her cervix and her womb removed so she never would carry her own child, but that herself and her partner wished to adopt. We talked deeply for a short time exchanging vital knowledge and experience, I of adoption. She gave wisdom, soothed and released my dirty, ashamed perceptions of cervical cancer.

I met Annette when she was picking up Jean from my house. She asked me if my adopted father was Mike Scally, I said he was. She told me that they had been colleagues and she remembered me as a child. After initial general stereotyping. I presumed her to be patronising and closed-minded and assumed she would think of me as the displaced, mixed-up generation of adopted adults. Annette and I sat down and reasoned. I realised after listening to her wisdom that she was the person who could show me a true sense of mind.

Annette did not take on my problems. Instead she shows me a path to my truth and helps me take my own breath. Her teachings helped me come to the realisation that I had been deceiving myself. My own sense of self felt drained but awake after the *Carnival Messiah*. I had to go back into hospital to have a second operation to remove more cancerous cells. My spirit felt low, I worried about my past and for my future. I worried about my relationship with my partner. If I couldn't have any more children, was it fair to carry on a relationship with a man who wanted to? The old issues I'd chosen to forget were surfacing like zombies. My teachings allowed me to see that I had not forgiven myself. Annette showed me how to cleanse my self from shame, blame, pain and guilt; to connect with my creator and move forward.

Annette taught me a history of birthright. I was told to visit aunties and uncles to acknowledge myself in my own destiny into my own family. I had read and heard a lot about the power of the name, but it had not clarified itself to me clearly until I had had my first session with Annette. Johnny, a poet and my friend, came to see me at my house. It was his first time in my home and he came laden with books of poetry and literature. The first book I picked up was by a woman named Cheryl Clarke; she was a Black woman from America. This poet resembled, smelled, had the same essence as me. It seemed exciting that I could be connected with family through poetry, through truth. When somebody talks your truth for the first time, it's like tasting your favourite food, the one that delights, caresses and fills your body. My realisations led me to believe in self and remove the labels and the issues.

\*\*\*

Myself, my mother and a few friends had never understood why, even as a young child, I felt the need to find my father, then my mother. How I seemed to adopt being Black. I remember being questioned by my adopted family if I said I was Black. This used to be a raging debate until the word Black became politically correct. I always thought I had to try hard not to be me, to suppress my passions, my desires, my spirituality, my reasoning, my memories, as others couldn't remember or never seemed to picture it in the same way. In hindsight I felt Black because that was my only true affirmation, nothing else was mine. In the children's home Michelle was Black and was very caring and warm. My birth father had seen me so it must have registered in my memory bank that I was Black.

I was still battling a truth in my identity. I had to sort out the guises and the masks from the truth. I was trying to maintain a positive relationship with all my parents but there were many things that I'd not forgiven. My spirit, I believe, was talking through my body and producing these pre-cancerous cells. There were a lot of things that I could value and admire in friends and community. As I opened to myself I found these people who I held to esteem, flowing and entering my world. Through our shared consciousness and support I felt my whole being healing. I would like to say a big thanks to the women friends Liz Powell,

Donneila, Michelle, Melanie, Lavina, Karen, Miriam, Ella, Judah, P, Marilyn and Annette, to the children, to God. We cried tears. We allowed for tears, laughter and reasoning. Our truth gathering as one, as it flowed with God. I am.

This is my story, everyone holds his or her own story, this is mine. My birth father loves me, I am an adult, his child. I am loved. It is a blessing to find so many Clarkes, so much family history, so much warmth and embracing. My adoptive family continues to give me the capacity to love, they gave me full freedom of speech in our talking. I thrive from their goodwill and am ready to put to use their skills and family values that apply to me. I believe. I honour my mothers and fathers and their union. I understand these feelings, for they have taught me too.

My uncle Danny is my birth father's brother. He is a truth, someone with whom I share an affinity with God, with spirit. I challenged my uncle with my truth of MotherGod and found he shared my sense of perception. All of my Clarke family hold up their truth. This is in God. This can also be in their vices, their monkeys. I see its clarity, truth in its whole is not always pleasant or nice, but it is real and you can always move from one sense of reality to another of realism. If you are given cover or protection over truth, then you do not have your sense of self to fight with. My sense of truth I've learnt does in fact pass through DNA, through ancestry back to God. I am just a student eager and, often, absently stupid but earnestly and honestly gifted. I can read my bloodline; spirit is mine. I respect and earn my position in my families to my God. The sins of my fathers I will and can be responsible for as an adult. This is not to walk in the pain or the madness but to bless and honour.

## Extract From Adoption Files

**4.9.72** Mrs Moran has been discharged from hospital. The nursing staff have little time for Mrs Moran. I wondered what she was running away from at this time and whether it could be contact with the children or whether this provoked guilt feelings, for she was imprisoned for their neglect at the time of their reception into care.

**18.9.72** Mrs Moran and Mr Clarke made arrangements to take the three Moran children at Easedale Close out for the day and wanted to take Michelle too. It was felt that they should visit the child a few more times before taking her out. Mr Clarke cannot accept Michelle is the responsibility of the department.

**29.9.72** Mr Clarke and Mrs Moran visit the children each Saturday.

**9.10.72** Mrs Moran did not visit the children Saturday and the children were very disappointed. Mrs Moran telephoned later and said that her mother had died last Friday and didn't want the children to learn of her death so suddenly

**8.11.72** Mrs Moran has promised the children treats and visits and being unable to afford just didn't turn up. The children were worried and just wanted to see her.

**8.12.72** Mrs Moran and Mr Clarke would like to arrange to have the children on Boxing Day. Arrangements were made.

**24.12.72** Took food parcel to Mrs Moran to help on Boxing Day. No one in so left with neighbour.

**29.12.72** Mrs Moran has slashed her wrists and thrown herself under a stationary lorry on the 23rd, so they couldn't collect the children on Boxing Day. The children were disappointed.

**6.2.73** Michelle was very upset at the prospect of leaving Miss Egan. I explained it might be the dark inside the car that she is afraid of. The children noticed a photo of Mr Clarke's daughter and this led to a long string of questions about his past marriage and why they couldn't all live together as a family again. Mrs Moran found the situation hard to cope with.

**7.2.73** Letter from Mrs Moran saying she did not want to see the children again.

## *Affirmation*

I am whole in my journey
I forgive myself for my journey
I thank God for her guides
I bless my friends and family
I honour my special relationships
I hold up, big up the community
To which I was born
I praise MotherGod
I walk in the reflection and
Dignity of myself and friends

## Vibes

Here is my spirit
Inside of my body
Make me give you
Sweet words to caress
Your spirit
I honour, before
My death
Just a speak easy reel
To make you relax
Everything about it
Feels in time
Like a lover
Or your baby's mind
Can you
Hear the Marley in my eyes?
I am him
In my womanly guise
Part of a spirit
Locked
Entwined
Here is my woman
Translates through my body
All to design
I give my first breath
Through living, bearing
The test and the rest
My womb is future's
Hard fall walk
My hands carved
To caress, to toil
Legs sturdy, to carry my head
Through jagged reality
In self times not met

Here I am, woman, mother
Grandmama maybe
Steeped and blessed
From cradle to creed
Here is the love
Celebration of life
I thank God
I felt the One Love vibe

## *Jah God*

At the top of the mountain
In the covenant of my being
Out of body, out of ghetto
Out of personal feeling
Releasing my destiny as my perception grows
The key to my Jah is to let others know
We are warriors of Jah, African princess
Bear we His fruit, we are MotherGod blessed
Spread His works, immersed in spiritual quest
Suckle His children 'pon our breast,
      Ingrain them with hidden memories of Africa blessed

We are warriors of Jah, no more, no less
We strive with vision we do our best
We cut the chains of possessiveness,
      Greed out of control
A weed in the field to the place we must go

Climb aboard Jah foot soldiers - lioness
Climb aboard ship sailing for his humanity quest
Feel the aura of Being Jah God Ness
African Princess
African Princess
      Smell the love sister, remove all our distress
           Be strong sister put our sisteren to the test
               Forgive your mother, your sister
                  your self and man
                    be ready for
                      JAH GOD
                      to hold your hand

## Spirit Poetry (Two)

And in the madness of my illiterate scrawl
And in the brandy-induced festival like brandy bowl
To You Jah I spell out the works to thee
In humbleness and security
You see
To know Jah feel the spiritual high
To know Jah know your African right
To know Jah lift your head with pride
    feel the vibe
'You nah have to run'
'You nah have to hide'
To see Jah greet your friends with glee
To see Jah speak to your enemies bout He
In praise Jah work with humanity
    feel the vibe
'For truth be written, Jah works be done'
'African people blessed as one'

## 1997, And I'm Glad To Be The Woman I've Become

I grew to know love, through my pain
I learnt from clarity, you will gain
Suffered humbling, but shone with pride
Like the new Africa

I WILL RISE

Two young lives born from within my womb
Love mentality they will bloom
Africa in my soul, my friends, the street
Fuel for intelligence to the tasks I meet

1997, Africa in my stride
There all along
Dis self respect made it hide
Chaos, trials meet with
Choice in peace of mind

I'm glad to be the woman I've become
I'm free to love
Not in pain
Trusting in clarity

We ALL will gain

## *Sanctuary*

I'm selfishly possessive of my sanctuary
Back off from the heat you see in my eyes
If you can't cook in the kitchen then you will fry
Negativity speaking is not where I lay
Godness works for godness
True thought is my plight
Try not break me
Break you, weaken your sap
Try not possess me, own me
You can't give me back
Don't cuss or scorn cause I hurt
Yours pride
A true friend am I, nothing to hide
Don't speak of my strength
With an argument
Nor look at my body
With only lustment
Collect Jah spirit
In strength in me
You can see me
Safely from my
Sanctuary

# The Sky's Her Eyes

*For Paula and Gary*

The sky's her eyes were forget-me-not blue
Did not think they could have shone so bright before
Wailed we grieved, tears of disbelief
Too much waste, in anger, face in such a short space of time
And did we heal the loss of mother from child

So the love comes in from the community
In times of forgotten need
Gather round and pray for peace

The sky's her eyes were forget-me-not blue
      Pierced with the dew
Did not think they could have pained to look no more
Too kind for this world, her pain endured
The road, the road
I think, that Jesus crawled
And did we feel the loss of mother from child
And did we heal the loss of mother from child
The skys her eyes were forget-me-not blue
And the pain, the pain
Broke like a damn
Tears of grief swam into tears of disbelief
Too much anger and waste
In such a short space of time
Did we feel the loss of mother from child
And did we heal the loss of mother from child

Stirred the love from the community
Hearts torn open, friends bereaved
Eyes of one of family
Swayed to the sisters sweet parting kiss
Sang, sang, to the Lord with so much force
That he took us by the hand.

## *Bright New Day*

It's a bright new day
It's on its way
It's okay

We're going to a bright new day
It's on its way
It's okay

Babies born and adults die
And the rain come through
And the self anewed
It's okay

I'm talking from my root's
I'm talking from the earth
Rebuilding in the seed
Seed of destiny
I walking in the pride
I talking in the time
I walking side by side
My God, myself, divine
I know the time is here
I know the time be true
I know you have to be
Be true to me
I know the time is here
I know the time is true
I lift my head a proud

Li Li Li Light

It's a bright new day
It's a bight new way
Its okay

And all the people say
And all the people's way
The money talk
The money fraud
And all the people sway
All the people wait
Armani talk
Armani fraud
And I walking with my eyes
Closed to the talking
And I walked with my eyes opened to God
It's the light
It shines so bright
From me to you
It's all done
True

Li Li Li Light

## My Flower

Leave me
Let me pick up
My petals that surround me
My waggered self
Annoys me
And you
For if were destiny
I'd have blossomed yesterday
Naked is not where
I chose to stay
Not anymore
A soul it has
To select being
For if I were
A bonsai tree
You'd preen and
Protect me
Be my gardener
With patient glee
Don't rake my soil
Or its chance to breathe
Single out
And tend to weed
Separate and protect
The seed
The seed of myself
Me
Or leave

## *Brighter*

*Bassy's song*

If every breath was you to keep me upright
If every thought of you brought powerment self guide
If every touch of you made make me soft silk like
If every thing in you is you then
Shine
Brighter than the biggest star
Man, in God, walk with me far
And feel the need in happiness
Restore our energy restlessness

To you I give to you what nobody has shared
To me you take me to the sense of I'm there
If death do part us then I shall be glad
To loved and lived with you 'til the righteous land

And woman
In God
Take me there
Prepare myself
In ritual we'll share
And shine

Brighter than the biggest star
In the dark of the velvet night
That first held our sight

And I know that we're there in God honey
In the strength of your warm caress
And I feel we're gonna be alright now darling
Lets leave the hype
Put ourselves to the test

## 9. Top of My Mountain

I am a proud Black woman of dual benefits and heritage. I present myself with thanks. I call on the whole of myself. I regain my own destiny. I am thus stronger and more able to nurture yours. Here is my spirit, here are my children. I am surrounded by a kin of sisters and brothers, aunties and uncles, cousins, birth and adopted. Here is my love, here is my spiritual wealth, here are my mentors, here is my, life my truth. These perceptions were made clearer by Annette. I give her thanks and appreciation. I believe I feel happy to see the world in my sense of truth. I follow the laws of God and ask for forgiveness when ego trips me up or when I chose to be bad because bad is much easier than good, than sticking to your truth in our fast, manipulating world of walls and lies. I accept life is not always a bed of roses. I understand my monkeys in life. I do not wish to judge but to seek knowledge, to avoid walking in the madness of other's monkeys. My spirit has moved away from that place and my path looks to be my own. I am coming out, I am a debutante, I baptise my woman through God in her sweet giving, giving her truth, her story and receiving in love.

I feel good, I feel at peace and I've stopped hurting; life continues its ever-turning circle. I meet up with communities of the past and walk forward into communities of the future. It has been a hard slog writing and rewriting. I have had to go back and heal many issues not only with myself but with my families. My inspirations and my peace feel full and overflowing. I feel blessed and privileged to be me here today. Writing this book to go with my poetry has forced me look at myself. Everything feels and tastes different now. My faith in the Holy MotherGod is bigger, stronger, more consuming and the light seems to be breaking through like the stars over an African desert night. My view on my adoption now is that this was my act of God. For at the top of my mountain this is what is shown. I am me and I like myself. My mum and dad loved me and put in unconditional commitment, responsibility, thought and patience. They loved me when I hated myself.

When I am sat around my Scally table and have all my brothers and sisters and beautiful nieces, cousins, aunties, uncles and friends enjoying the conversation and loving the company of each other then I have to sit back in awe of myself and my family. For the six-year-old who came to the Scallys would have never recognised the woman in peace or mother she has become. I love being Michelle Scally. I love the fact that my brothers and sisters are all different, the stimulation and friendship and support from them is independent and gentle. I no longer feel inferior to them and I wish also to thank them for staying gentle and strong for their sister. One love, I think, is communicated by the question, am I my brother's keeper? The answer, I hear from my Scallys is, yes, you are. The lining of my wealth and well-being is the soil from which I have grown, The Scallys.

Who am I like? Am I like my birth family? That is a question that travelled with me until I met my Clarke family. The answer would be, in many ways, yes. My spirit jumps when I see any of my Clarke relations. It is happy and comforting to be in the company of them. I am able to study their patterns and family, and from the grounding and patterns from the Scally family, I am able to work myself and my emotions and thoughts out; this brings peace. When I see the strong Clarke females I recognise myself as one of them. My veils of hurt and insecurity I have lifted from my eyes and feel like I have woken from a cocoon, from a soul depression. I have the sun shining and feel adult or like a butterfly, light, confident, and ready to die. I'm climbing on a natural high, up my mountain. My writing, poetry, music and workshops feel stimulating and relevant. I feel it comes from God, to me it is God-given to be able to look at life from a third point of view and to then be able to communicate it in words and song with a band or on a theatre stage. I am blessed to even live my dream and give more than thanks to my friends, partners and musicians that support and live our dreams.

My CIN scare is over, I am still able to conceive. I move forward to the future with my children happily at the moment, being very, very single. Aerron and I, as Shâme, have travelled overseas giving poetry and music workshops to schools. I think this kind of work really helps to heal. When I am working in a classroom or in a group, I get flashbacks of the really good teachers such as Mrs Cockeram and Mr Gibbons, my drama and history teachers, and giggle quietly inside when I think of the shock they would have seeing me up here. Then I open myself up just like they did and allow the pupils to feel and acknowledge my spirit and presence before asking them of theirs. I hope the young people and adults that I have worked with have the same taste of memory that I have when I think of them.

I love to express song, stories, jazz, blues, romance, dub, bingy and, occasionally, politics with my poetry. I look at the emotion behind and pick up either the bassline of one of the instruments, such as the violin or sax and then, in my mind's eye, I start to dance with it, like a waltz or a salsa. Then I pick up my thought of the day and we begin making music. Aerron and I, and now Roisin, who has joined us (we met Roisin when she booked us for her gig at the Edinburgh Festival, called *Recognition*) have a great telepathic communication going. Our work is bouncing off each other all the time, and our inspirations and dreams connect. We are all in, or nearly in, the 30-something bracket, and our relationship has the advantage of being adult and professional. I think we empower each other and we certainly feel like we create magic when we are together. Sometimes Aerron will have written some music then Roisin, who lives in Scotland, and myself will have also independently written some lyrics or poetry. It is a real buzz when they fit like pieces of a jigsaw puzzle.

The band and I have been working together for a year-and-a-half now and I feel privileged to work alongside people I choose as friends. Richard, the double-bass player, and I have a good relationship going with my emotion and his bass. Richard lives in Chapeltown, not far from me, and it is my therapy, almost, to be able to walk to his house after a stressful day and sing my blues or hit the jazz. Paulette and Annette believed in me from the first moment. We take time to listen to each other's worries or hurdles that everyday life throws up. I love it when they sing with me, I get a feeling-alive buzz, a smiley, happy buzz, one that tastes innocent and real good fun, just like childhood. Chris, the guitarist, is another one of my mentors. Chris reminds me of my son. His mind is astute and focused, his thoughts are precise and owned. When he plays his guitar you are able to see his spirit. He is very much like a big brother and feels no way about telling me off or reminding me to stay calm. He has empowered Aerron and myself in faith and belief for our future. Farouq is a drummer, he doesn't speak much but then he doesn't have to as his eyes and expressions let you know exactly how he is. I asked Farouq to write about himself and he said, 'I am a drummer not a singer.' Farouq can be my drummer through any of my journeys because I trust him. He trusts himself, which makes his presence in the band strong and valued.

My album is a collaborated infusion of spirit poetry and music. My friends and musicians worked hard to support myself and Aerron empowering us and believing in us. They help to make life a bigger, richer memory, I feel so humbled and honoured by their wisdom and experience, these are people who continue the foundation of community, they put back in what they have taken out, they are Marley warriors, Jah goodness. It worries me that I may leave something out when reliving memories back to the page, so this is them, in their words.

## I Am **Aerron Davydd Perry**

I have faith and believe
I see my path before me unfold
Page by page
I am one particle in one atom in one cell

In one family
I observe and listen
I distil and nurture
I walk with my friends
Our collaborations reflect on truth
One truth
The more I uncover
The more I see
The more I see
The more I grow

I Am **Paulette Joseph**
I am compelled by passion
It stands me to attention
I love singers and players of instruments
Thriving off energy that pulls both ways
I no longer believe
That I have control
Over my passions
I give it up to God

I Am **Chris Campbell**
Seed of my mother and father
Child of creation
Child of the earth, the universe
I am just one of the voices in the choir
The ensemble
One of the strands in the weave
Happy to be so
I hope this can help to bring happiness to even one
Praise the creator

I Am **Richard Bostock**
I am usually quiet
Or unusually quiet

But I have a voice
I want others
To give voice
We listen

I Am **Annette**
Here is my spirit
I give from my spirit
To my music
My connection of God
Is like moving waking
A place where I want to go
I am a mother
In love
With my children
My God
Myself
My music
My passion
I live a story
That has not been told
And my inner strength
Guides
And in my faith
I know
My time will come
I give my love
To the inspiration
That brought all this together
Respect due
To one and all

I am **Farouq Abdullah Husain**
Drummer...silent...strong...keeper of time
Ironic, given that it's only time that I don't have

Time is not within my power
Neither can I advance it nor throw it down
Time is a gift, bestowed upon us by the almighty creator
Formed, and loaned to us
I GUESS WE ALL LIVE ON BORROWED TIME
Precious...it is not to be wasted
It is the very basis of our being
With time, we create rhythms, movement, sound and shapes
Rhythms that have been with us since the first Afrikkan
And that tradition has passed on through the hands
That have influenced mine...
Time witnessed the 500 year destruction of my people
Who's 100 million souls cry out
'My youth my youth...remember our time!'
Should I dishonour them, by living here, today
And wasting my time?
Honour them
Honour me
Be on time

\* \* \*

I received my files from Catholic Care. I could not trace my birth mother before as I had not received her proper date of birth, they were on the files. My mother, Margaret Theresa Watson was born 18th November. What knowledge I received from the files affirmed my character and my personality. My files say that I was 'deaf, subnormal' for the first two-and-a-half years of my life. This must have been when I met God. It is very important for me to leave you, the reader, with the very clear conclusion that I am blessed, I am a survivor and I will continue to stumble, flourish and make my way to the top of my mountain, with my love to my MotherGod and my mothers, being the women who loved love and can be seen calling and teaching from the top of their mountains. Thanks to Mum, Aunty Maureen, my godmother, Everlina, Greta, Joan, and my Clarke Aunties, Olive, Melvina, Claretta, Doris, Immelda, my sisters and friends, aunty Carmel Egan, granny Betty Scally Bates. As all of them is all you'll find, woman leaves her scent behind.

*Here is my spirit*
*I can bring it into view*
*I can look and see where my paths will lead*
*I have enough life lessons and empowerment*
*I believe in God and in light*
*I believe in my laughter and my love*
*I believe in my poetry*
*In my children*
*In  myself*
*I believe because my spirit is known and received*
*I am received in spirit, in skin back to my family called Clarke*
*My journey is now mine*
*This is my time*
*My labels lay among me like yesterday's clothes*
*Here is my spirit*
*It is shouting light gulping in positive affirmation*
*To a once negative abused mind*
*It has been a difficult and rewarding journey*
*My life my families, my children in God*
*I am full and rich in this wealth*
*Here is my spirit alive and healing*
*I lay a prayer at the top of truth's head*
*I pray a blessing and thanks to my friends and mentors*

# Extract From Adoption Files

**10.8.73** Michelle was being used as a pawn between Mum and Dad

**12.73** Summary. Mrs Moran has disappeared from the home taking with her belongings to Mr Clarke and he intends prosecuting.

**20.2.74** Michelle is quite a young woman now, she is attached to the staff at Millgreen, as they are to her, and she is going to find it very hard when she leaves. She is very fosterable and in the light of her mother's disappearance I feel we should seek a foster home for her in order for her to be settled before she starts school.

**8.74** Summary. Michelle enjoys her trips to see the other Moran children, though these only occur about every two months.

**25.11.74** As it is planned that Michelle be introduced into a foster home I feel that it would be helpful for Michelle's ties at Millgreen to be loosened.

**1.75** Summary. Michelle is very petted at the children's home and I think might well become quite precocious.

**24.6.75** Michelle sleeps with Michelle Rabjohn and is almost a sister to Sean Morrison. Possible fostering fallen through, Michelle suitable for adoption. Mrs Moran has resurfaced in Bradford, she wants to see other children but not Michelle.

**8.75** Mrs Moran has no wish to see Michelle and said she would give consent for adoption. I have spoken about this and this is a relief though her colour is an embarrassment.

**4.76** Michelle attends St Gregory's School. She is badly in need of an adoptive home but correct selection is important. Catholic Rescue recently suggested a possible family and were very pressing that we should take it up. The Adoptions Section and myself felt it unsuitable as (1) there was no contact with colour in the family or area and (2) an adopted child would not be the youngest. Miss Egan disagreed and felt we should try this family rather than delay any longer. It is true that placement becomes more difficult as Michelle gets older. She no longer sees other Moran children and does not ask to do so.

**6.9.76** Michelle moves to the Scally House.

**27.5.77** Adoption order made, Michelle discharged from care.

## Blessing

A blessing goes out to the liburd
I've protection for my flight
I owe an honourance of forget-me-not
I'll love you when you cry

I call goes out to the liburd
I'll fly high, from your song
A remembrance in forget-me-not
I was born to sing my song

## *Marley Tribute*

Children are crying
Their truth is lying
Hole in the mission
A vague contradiction
   Yeah


All I ever have, All I ever have, All I ever have


Drugs and their losers
Cocaine, Champagne abusers
NATO's death missions
Adult's loss, children's vision
    Yeah


All I ever have, All I ever have, All I ever have


We have our church of abusers
Blood, war, guilt fuses
We have air in our right
You can't win war with fight
    No


All I ever have, All I ever have, All I ever have


I have my friends and my humour
I have my kids I'm a mother
I have love of above
I thank Marley love
    Yeah


All I ever have, All I ever have, All I ever have

# Salt Of Tears (The Windrush poem)

Do you know why the sea has salt?
I can taste it in my eyes
In the rush
In her tide

A celebration in commemoration
Of a new Caribbean nation
1948, June 22nd
Ship in sailing, promises waiting
500 baited, their courage their tool
Self-sacrifices
Economic crises, racist propaganda
In a political agenda

Power in fear, grains of fact
Working to gain, hiding the pain

Do you know why the sea has salt?
Drops from my eyes
We owe our wisdom, our ancestral line
We the first generation have to reap from their grind

British Black nation
Has not our blood bled for British men?
Three generations of West Indian foundation
Government manipulation
Is not our lie

In the rush
In her tide
If a few
Were so many
How many is a few

Can we honour, withstand in truth?
So with jubilation
I a product of a courageous mass migration
In Windrush celebration
Aware that the salt
Of your tears
Kept me alive

## *Sounds of Truth*

Sing for our slaves
Who died for us
Who suffered in the trust
That we, we would rise
Again, not fight
Fight, in pain
Drop hate, rise
Again, African friend
True Carrib descendant
Access deep in the mind
True computer you
Will find
In our first millennium
Our work has begun
Our minds open
To lessons that should
Have been learnt
Before our time
Time was denied
In our minds, physical strength
We must implement
Our views which
The west took as rules
Time to pay our
Birth dues
Lead
Again
The
Misguided men

## *Shâme*

*[sh~a:m] f. soul; mind; 1. People with different shâme, coming together to create a sound borne out of different loves; 2. Call it what you want call it shâme.*

Your programming is now not my waste of time
      shâme
If you choose to ferment into the cocoons
You call security
      shâme
Not in the higher knowledge of your mind
      shâme
Don't come find me
DON'T waste your time
      shâme

I'm finished with the ego attitude
You protrude
      shâme
I'm down with self
As I choose to move
      shâme
Your glass~house para
Is now not of time
      shâme

It's late
It's sad
Don't waste your time

Come, come look at me
If you've got nothing to lose
      shâme

In the sins in we
I'll pay my dues
          shâme
I'm down with the sanity
Of my being
With the God-given right
To love
To feel
SO
If my words
Don't ring the rhyme
Don't come find me
Don't waste your time
          shâme